BRAND LEGACY

MAKE YOUR MARK

Thanks for your support

Angela Mayartis Johnson

~Make Your Mark on the World~

.Mayartis J.

Mayartis Inc.

*This book is dedicated to the loving memory
of my grandmother, Phyllis Adele Beckles, who
lived her life as an avid prayer warrior always
serving others. While she was here,
she kept me safe with her prayers and now
she's my guardian angel, watching over me.
I miss and love her dearly.*

TABLE OF CONTENTS

ACKNOWLEDGEMENTS

Writing this book has been an incredible introspective journey that has forced me to dig deep and prove to myself that not only do I have something to say, but that what I have to say needs to be heard — in my own voice. I truly have to thank my mother, Margot Williams, for helping me to achieve this milestone, because she taught me how to be strong and repeatedly told me that I could accomplish anything or do anything that I set my mind to. She has always supported me, even when she may not have understood the reason(s) for my (at times) crazy decisions. However, she knew that the moment I resolved do something, I would somehow make it happen and she was always there to lend a helping hand.

To my amazing friends, I express my deepest and heartfelt thanks for providing encouragement to me in so many ways. You have connected me with the right people when I needed guidance, met me for a delicious meal when I needed a break (everyone knows I love to eat), offered essential feedback to enhance the book and pushed me to complete it, even when I didn't see an end in sight. I am thankful to each and every one of you, and I will forever be grateful for your love and support.

Thanks to my extraordinary editor, Steven Chean, who helped bring my words to life; my book cover designer, Redondo Rabago, of Visual Taboo, who is a creative genius; and my photographers, Stephanie Hayes of Stephanie Allen Photography and Darren Williams, who always found the perfect shot.

Most importantly, I thank God for each and every blessing, because I know He is working within me, around me, and through me. I believe that God has a well-designed plan for me and for this book, and that I am only an instrument of His work. Thank you, Lord, for using me.

PREFACE

August 15, 2014 was designated to be my last day as an employee. On that day, I was to begin pursuing my passion, living my purpose, and accomplishing my life's goals. I was leaving a job that I enjoyed at one time, but now it only met an essential need — paying my bills. My job afforded me the ability to travel the country, stay in amazing hotels and eat at the finest restaurants. However, I was now bored out of my mind, because I was not doing what I was meant to do with my life.

My passions revolved around my desire to help professional athletes to define their brand and use it to transition from their current career to the next chapter of their lives. I wanted to travel the world and talk to students, encouraging them to cultivate a goal-oriented mindset that would help them move into their first career or launch their own business. I wanted to help those in need develop a personal-branding/goal-setting mentality that would inspire them to define their purpose, pursue their passion, and live their life . . . *now*.

But for the time leading up to the August 1st date, I was content to merely pay my bills. So, I continued to build my business while working at my 9-to-5, all the while hoping to sign a big client and announce my resignation. No such luck. My situation became a joke among a few of my coworkers: I had told them that as soon as I got my business together, I would leave. However, each of them left before me, for better paying jobs. I was adamant that I would not leave the company to go work for anyone else. I would resign only to work for myself. But the money, the perks, and the ability to build my business while I paid my bills with ease were hard to abandon. Then, one day, it happened: I chose my end-date and put my exit plan in motion.

I experienced something I branded Parallel Career Metamorphosis – the journey on which one embarks, while transitioning out of their then-current position. This process birthed *Brand Legacy* — a guide for those who dream of something more than their current occupation, and are considering a change from their present physical and/or mental circumstances to their intended future. As we all know, stepping into the unknown is simultaneously exciting and terrifying, but understanding the process makes the journey a little easier and far more rewarding.

Although anyone can glean insight from this book, I focus on helping:

1. Professional athletes, because too many of them have lost everything after a promising career. We put

elite athletes on a pedestal, yet we never help them to cultivate their other talents and achieve their remaining goals.

2. Students, because if we help them to create a goal-oriented mindset before they enter the workforce, their chances of leaving a tremendous legacy while positively impacting the world are greatly improved.

3. Employees: those looking to take their career to the next level or change it completely, because they are unhappy or bored in their current position.

Through the use of Brandercises (branding exercises), vivid real-life stories and key transitional tips, *Brand Legacy* will educate readers on how to understand their value proposition in order to accomplish their dreams. It will teach them how to become dynamic leaders and change their community for the better. It will instruct them how to live a passion-filled, purpose-driven life and leave a legacy that communicates their narrative.

Chapter 1

PCM

"The goal of personal branding is to be recruited based on your brand, not applying for jobs."
— *Dan Schawbel*

You may have spent every waking moment developing your skills in a specific career, and although you are heading towards the peak of your profession, you know in the back of your mind that this period will not last forever and you desire to do more. But what and how? You are building a valued brand in your chosen field, but you have other goals and aspirations that you have pushed aside to accomplish your first passion. It is as though you have woken up from a great dream (your current life), but you feel as though there's more — more that you could be doing, more that you *want* to be doing.

Think about it: You have built an incredible brand as an athlete throughout your entire life, or you have been a solid student succeeding in certain courses, or you're a rising star at your company . . . However, you yearn to utilize some of your other talents. But how do you do that while continuing to thrive where you are? You begin by deciding you want more and acting on it. By doing your very best and becoming an expert in your field. By defining your goals and creating a strategic plan to accomplish them. By using a process called Parallel Career Metamorphosis (or PCM) to help you live a new life. What is PCM?

Parallel Career Metamorphosis is the process or period of transformation from one stage in your career to another via thorough self-examination, definition of your life's purpose, creation of a detailed plan, results-oriented actions, and determination to see the transition take place.

Parallel Career Metamorphosis (or **PCM**) will help you to accomplish the following:

- ☛ Build financial security for you and your loved ones.

- ☛ Secure peace of mind regarding your future.

- ☛ Accomplish the other goals you have been considering.

- ☛ Create an additional stream of income while you are still in your present occupation.

PCM is not a plan B, but the achievement of one of your many goals in life. Oftentimes we assume anything that is not our first goal is a plan B. But stating that something is a plan B assumes that we failed a plan A, when, in fact, we have accomplished all that we possibly could in achieving that goal and are moving on to the next goal on our lifelong list.

Our parents were told to choose a career and excel at it in order to become a valued commodity to their employer; in turn, the employer would acknowledge them with promotions, raises, augmented responsibilities, and potential job security. However, the employer-employee loyalty that our parents so enjoyed is no longer a reality. Employees move from company to company in order to maximize financial and career growth. Equally, employers hire and fire employees today much quicker and for many reasons, including:

1. Company reorganization due to profit loss

2. Mergers and acquisitions

3. Lack of updated technology

4. Downsizing to save business

5. Change of business model

If you have not been downsized, fired, or laid off due to one of the above, then you most likely know someone who has. However, there are rare cases of people like my mother, who is what I call a "job lifer" — someone who has the same job for their entire adult life. As a child she wanted to be a nurse, so she attended nursing school in England, and upon graduation received a job at Brigham and Women's Hospital in Boston, from which she retired in 2013. In other words, my mom had one job at one company. How many of you can happily claim as much? She received yearly increases, advance degree education, and token gifts every time she surpassed another goal-year working at the company. This was an ideal situation for her, because she was doing what she loved while supporting her family, and she still had time to vacation and volunteer at church and other organizations. Such a life is perfect for the person with only one career goal. But if you have other career plans, then you need to consider PCM.

The premise of PCM is built on creating goals. If you take the time to sit down and write out all of your goals (and I believe everyone should do this), you will have a lifetime of things to accomplish and it will keep your days interesting and exciting. PCM is not a plan B, but the middle ground between being a student and being self-employed, between being a professional athlete and developing a business, or being an employee maneuvering between employers to achieve various career aspirations. PCM will help to extend your financial career and build a legacy after you have achieved your first goal. PCM is so important because very few people have the financial ability, knowledge, experience, or support system to guide them as they decide that they are going to leave their current company to become an entrepreneur or drop out of school to start a business overnight. Those who have the necessary tools to leave their current position may not be ready to say goodbye to their first goal. Saying goodbye to something you have worked toward for most of your life is difficult. There are also those who do not have the necessary knowledge to change careers or start a business. So what do you do?

If you were at the peak of your career, earning an

unimaginable salary doing what you loved and everything was as perfect as it could be, but there were potential health issues, would you retire/quit to achieve your next goal? Former Detroit Lions running back Billy Sims was forced to retire from the NFL after only five seasons. During that time, he amassed more than 5,000 rushing yards while being voted into the Pro Bowl three times. And if those achievements were not enough, he helped the Lions reach the playoffs in both 1982 and 1983.

But his career ended abruptly in 1984, when he endured a severe knee injury. What was he to do now that his first goal was behind him? Initially, his retirement was difficult financially, as he had made some bad deals and investments, including stakes in a radio station, a dinette manufacturer, a mini-supermarket, a nightclub, and an apartment complex. These failures forced him into bankruptcy, which sent his life into a tailspin. Fortunately, he was able to turn things around by licensing the use of his name to a barbecue restaurant and becoming vice president of a non-profit organization, AmericaCan.

Sims did the right thing in trying to secure his legacy by investing in various businesses. Unfortunately, they were not the right ones. Although he may have vetted the companies, risk is an inevitable part of investment — and a huge part of being an entrepreneur. His career ended before he was ready. As a result, he was unprepared to transition. Imagine if his investments had panned out as he was working on his career — he would have been set financially and could have used his assets to further develop his legacy.

The consummate executive chameleon, Sean John Combs (Puff Daddy, P. Diddy), is a prime example of a student who had several goals and set out to accomplish all of them. In high school he was immersed in hip-hop culture, hanging out at radio stations where emerging artists were trying to get airplay, and in clubs where many of the same artists were honing their skills. It was then, at a time when he was not even of legal age to enter those clubs, that he knew he wanted to be a dancer, producer, artist, and music industry executive.

He realized his first dream by dancing in music videos for Doug E. Fresh, and Stacy Lattisaw, before heading off to Howard University to pursue a degree in business management. Sean had an entrepreneurial mindset and from a young age hustled to make money. He launched his first company, A Black Man and a Puerto Rican Production, with schoolmate Deric Angelettie. Together they promoted parties, their first including then-up-and-coming Heavy D, Slick Rick, Doug E. Fresh, and Guy. It was their first of many well-attended, start-studded events.

Sean continued his studies at Howard, but he was focused more on making a name for himself and his brand, although he may not have called it that at the time. He drove four hours into the Manhattan to look for employment in the music industry. When no one hired him, he reevaluated the situation and sought an internship instead. He used his connection with Heavy D, by then an artist on Andre Harrell's label, Uptown Records, to speak to Harrell about an internship.

Sean worked at the Uptown office two days a week, which meant that he traveled to New York City from Washington, D.C. (a four-hour drive each way) to complete tedious tasks with other college interns, with hopes that his efforts would, lead to a job. He made sure to take copious notes, and if someone needed something — especially Andre — he would have it to them faster and better than anyone else (building that brand). In other words, he worked hard and made sure that everyone knew who he was, what he did, and what he could do, so when there was an opportunity to move into the Artist & Repertoire department, he got it.

Sean continued to make smart moves throughout his life in order to accomplish his dreams. As he achieved one set of goals, he created a new one — always excelling in one area in order to help him transition successfully to another. Sean Combs is prime example of PCM at work.

PCM helps those ready to achieve a new goal prepare for the next phase in their life. If you are ready to begin your transformation from where you are to where you are planning to go, then you are ready to begin your PCM journey.

1. Be open to the journey.
2. Understand what a personal brand is, its impact, and how to create it.
3. Develop a Personal Brand Mindset.
4. Secure a mentor and accountability partner to help you with the process.

5. Determine your goals/purpose/*why*.

6. Devise your brand.

7. Communicate your story.

8. Manage the perception.

9. Transition to entrepreneur/new job.

10. Impact your community — give back!

Chapter 2

The Authentic You

"Be so good they can't ignore you."

— *Steve Martin*

Personal branding is the authentic YOU.

Personal branding is how people engage and experience YOU.

Personal branding is how people know and feel about themselves through YOU.

Personal branding is people's perception of YOU.

PCM works on the premise of creating a personal brand that is highly sought after in any area. In other words, create such a strong identity that employers, teams, and clients are begging you to join them. With that in mind, before you begin the process of PCM you must understand what a personal brand is and how to maximize it to seek everything you want out of life. A personal brand is like a one-person play, in which you are the writer, actor, and director. The writer creates an award-winning script (a documentation of who you are), develops the play (you developing your brand), does the

set design, wardrobe, and marketing (you or your team communicating your brand to your potential audience), performs
the play onstage (the action in your life) for the audience (the
world) to experience.

The audience then develops its own interpretation of the
play, which may or may not be congruent with your thought
process. After the play, as you interact with the audience, you
have a chance to learn about their opinions and possibly change
them based on your engagement (this is brand management).
Our personal brands are others' perception of us based upon
information that we may or may not have supplied them, as
opposed to our perception of ourselves.

Have you ever seen the photo of a little girl looking in a
mirror and seeing a reflection of herself as a princess, or the
kitten whose reflection is a lion? How do you see yourself
when you look in the mirror? What is your perception verses
your reality? You may be asking yourself, *If my brand is what
people see and not exactly whom I see myself as, then why build
a brand? People will think what they want to think.* The answer:
If you do not build your brand, others will build it for you;
in the process, maybe they will build an incorrect image of
you — the *you* that's currently known among friends, family,
and coworkers. To build your brand, you must take a deep,
honest look inside yourself to see where you are and determine what you need in order to get where you want to go.
In the process you'll be answering a lot of questions about
yourself. If you answer them honestly, you should be able to

create an amazing brand. The four key components of your personal brand are:

- ✔ **Image:** physical appearance, wardrobe, tattoos, piercings, body language.

- ✔ **Persona**: emotional qualities that differentiate you from other people.

- ✔ **Proficiencies**: skillset — things that you do extremely well due to experience or training.

- ✔ **Beliefs**: faith or confidence in someone or something that helps to define what you say and do.

Each of these points plays a significant role in crafting your personal brand, so go over each and determine how you view yourself. We will delve into each of these points throughout the book in order to define and develop your brand. Below are a few initial questions that you should ask yourself to help unveil your brand:

- ☞ How would you describe yourself?

- ☞ What is your image saying about you?

- ☞ What is your persona and how is it perceived by those with whom you engage?

- ☞ Are your proficiencies well known in your personal and business lives?

- ☞ What are your core beliefs?

At first glance these questions seem quite easy. And they are, if you have already done an intense self-examination or if your responses are surface answers. What do I mean by "surface answers"? Answers that fail to probe into who you are at the core. Oftentimes when we are not confident in our brand, we have a representative who does the initial greeting. This representative is the part of our persona that everyone loves. But it's not the real you. You choose to not show the real you until you are comfortable with the person and/or your brand.

It's similar to the person you meet at a networking event. They have a great business card, an informative website, and all the right answers. But then you get to know them. You suggest a partnership or other business opportunities that are in line with their profession, but they always seem to have an excuse as to why they can't do it or why their own business is stagnant. You begin to ask questions and come to find out that outside of the website and other branding materials, they have done nothing to build their business. You are disappointed, because you thought this was a great contact. Then you begin to feel sad, because this person who has great promise is too scared to act on the thing they truly desire.

I sent a prospective client a list of questions similar to those above, so that we could determine where he was with his brand. Unfortunately, he was unable to write down answers to the questions. It was not that he was unable to *answer* the questions; rather, it was that the act of writing them down made him think about the answers more deeply than he was prepared to think. When I asked him the question verbally, he responded with a vague but terrific-*sounding* answer. However, when he took some time to dig deep, he not only discovered a wealth of things that he did not realize were there, but also a deeper, stronger passion for the things he really wanted to work on. It helped him to discover his *why*. Taking the time to think deeply about what you are passionate about and why you are passionate about it helps you to discover the real you. Find out things about yourself that you did not consider a key part of your brand or things others see in you that you do not see in yourself. In other words, why onlookers' image of you is different than your image of yourself.

The questions above, combined with a few more detailed ones, will help you to take a more profound look at who you are personally and professionally. From there you can determine what you need to do to get where you want to go.

Chapter 3

Brand Impact

> "What makes you unique makes you successful."
> — *William Arruda*

A **personal brand can be created for a student, an** athlete, and an employee — anyone looking to expose him or herself to a particular demographic for financial, emotional, spiritual, or physical gain.

After you devise and develop your brand, you'll use marketing to communicate it to the world. Marketing is used to build awareness, introduce customers, and boost sales. If you were a company, you would market your brand to consumers and possibly other companies, but as a personal brand you'll market to employers, clients, teams, schools, and anywhere else that caters to your personal brand.

All well-known brands are built over time by understanding their strengths and weaknesses, utilizing them to effectively establish their name. A clear, concise message will help to make you stand out among the crowd. Superman, The Answer, and Prime Time are professional athletes who were born with the names Brandon Barnes, Allen Iverson, and Deion Sanders, respectively. Why were they branded with these nicknames?

Barnes received his moniker because of his incredible leaping ability on the baseball field. Allen Iverson was called The Answer because his being drafted by the Philadelphia 76ers came in response to the following questions: Who's our guy? Who's going take us to the NBA Finals? Who will put Philly back on the NBA map? Meanwhile, Prime Time was the perfect name for a man who played football and baseball — the only athlete ever to hit a home run and score a touchdown within a seven-day period.

Their names were given to them based on the things they did to excel in their respective sport(s). Sanders was blessed with outstanding athletic skills and an aggressive confidence that annoyed some but attracted many others to his brand. Whether you loved him or hated him, Prime Time proved his worth in the MLB and NFL by helping to lead his teams to the World Series and the Super Bowl. He definitely lived up to his name. Can you live up to the name you are building for yourself, or do you need to define/redefine your brand? These athletes were given nicknames that expressed their talents, personas, or positions. The average person will not have a nickname by which the world knows them, but they will be known by their brand, which is the name their parents gave them.

Understanding your brand impact is the difference between people knowing your name versus knowing your name and how it affects them. This comes into play particularly when you are looking for a job, trying to make an impact on a team, or even getting into school. Your brand and, more importantly, the ability to communicate your brand are essential. People want to believe in brands that share their values and meet their expectations. If your brand can make an impact on their team, at their school, or within their company, then they want you.

By understanding your brand impact and articulating it effectively, you can be assessed and warmly embraced by fans, a company, a team, customers, and a community that believe in and even share your values. Knowing your own brand means that you can sell it more efficiently and distinguish a market that will accept/buy it. Knowing that a student, athlete, entertainer, employee, or entrepreneur has a certain value is great, but it's not enough: You need to show it in your actions. Knowing your *why*, embracing your *purpose*, and understanding how both influence and form your attitudes, actions, and interactions enables you to make better strategic decisions when pursuing your goals.

In the 2013 NFC Championship Game, the Seattle Seahawks battled the San Francisco 49ers to see who would earn the right to go to the Super Bowl. In the last few minutes of a very close game, Richard Sherman tipped a Colin Kaepernick pass intended for Michael Crabtree in the end zone. Linebacker Malcolm Smith picked it off, clinching the Seahawks' second trip to the Big Game. As with most post-game broadcasts, the player who made the most significant impact was interviewed, and this day was no different, as the high-spirited Sherman exuberantly exclaimed, "I'm the best corner in the game! When you try me with a sorry receiver like Crabtree, that's the result you gonna get."

His remarks set off a social media firestorm in which he was labeled crazy, ignorant, and several other unflattering names not so much for what he said as the way he said it. The next day several Forbes.com contributors, including Tommy Tomlinson, gave us deeper insight into Sherman — namely that he graduated second in his high school class before graduating from Stanford with a degree in communications, "which might explain why, while he *seemed* to be hollering like a crazy person, he didn't curse once and looked into the camera the whole time." The article also reminded us that when Sherman sat down with Fox NFL a few hours later, he was "calm and funny."

The initial interview took place within five minutes of the game-winning play. Sherman knew he was going to the Super Bowl and was extremely excited. We all show our excitement in different ways. Sherman's adrenaline was pumping, hence his over-exuberant response. Did this incident help or hurt his brand? Did he speak out of turn and garner the additional publicity accidentally or was it a keen branding ploy that might land him an endorsement? Whether his animated response was planned or a happy accident, he capitalized on an opportunity and impacted his brand. Hopefully, he has put together a winning marketing team that can use this extra time in the spotlight to pick up additional sponsors, as well as repair any brand damage incurred as a result of the interview.

A brand can be the catalyst that makes one person stand

out, but if the person fails to live up to their brand, it could be a crucial downfall. Athletes who develop brands based on their ability do so to safeguard their position on their teams and, hopefully, help them secure sponsorships. As students and professionals, you do the same thing, because you receive a job due to your perceived skillset, experience, and other online marketing — not via TV or other press.

Chapter 4

Get Your Mind Right

"Changing the game is a mindset."
— *Robert Rodriguez*

I n order to effectively establish a lasting brand, you must develop a mindset that you *are* a brand and not just a person. Evolving into having a personal branding mindset is a key component of PCM.

It does not mean that you become another person or that you are self-centered. It means that you are highlighting the things you want others to know about you in order to drive home your brand. Prime Time used his exceptional skills on the field to get to the NFL. He used his marketing ability to expose his brand, which, in turn, helped him stay in the game as well as extend his career to sports broadcasting. His brand even garnered him a couple of successful reality shows. In short, he developed the mindset that he was not just a person or a superstar athlete — he was a brand that could leverage sponsorships, additional jobs, and a host of other things.

To change your mindset you have to change your thinking from negative to positive. It seems to be a learned behavior to hold onto everything you do poorly and disregard the things you do well. In order to build your desired brand you must change your negative thoughts and develop your positive thoughts. Do it by remembering those negative experiences, and how they impacted you and those around you. Negative thought-recall comes in handy when the event helped you to create a positive memory. If you lost a job, but it helped you to focus on starting your business, then that was a negative thought that positively affected you. J.K. Rowling turned her negative circumstances into a positive by doing what she loved. Raising her daughter by herself while surviving on social security, she wrote her first novel, *Harry Potter and the Philosopher's Stone*. Today she's internationally known for her *Harry Potter* fantasy series as well as for being the first person to become a billionaire from writing. How is that for changing your negative into a positive? She completely turned her dire situation into a historic success story. We all have that power within us — we just have to tap into it and have the perseverance to make it happen.

In creating a personal brand you have to understand and embrace your weaknesses in order to counteract them. If one of your weaknesses is finance, budgeting, or accounting, but you are great at marketing, highlight your skills in marketing and then mention how your innovative concepts helped the company's bottom line, ultimately bringing the conversation back to the numbers. If you are starting a business, make sure that you hire or contract a financial wiz to deal with your cash flow and budgets, so you are covered when creating the business's big-picture plan. Bringing someone in to maintain the cash flow will also make you look good to investors. If you are going for a job, your ideal position would be marketing-based and you would hire someone who is skilled at budgets.

In developing your personal brand, you must look past your perceived shortcomings and start building based on strengths. This process might take a while, because we have to relearn to not invest in our negatives since they can hold us back. We're not living up to our potential because we're constantly saying (and believing), "I don't have the people around me," "I lack the needed financial resources," or "I lack the knowledge," when in actuality we have everything we need to get started, and everything else will come in time. In order to craft a strong, timeless brand, you must change your negative brand mindset into an "I can do anything I put my brand to" mindset. To make this happen, your brand must:

1. **Be unique** — Flying under the radar is not acceptable. You must make sure your audience sees how you stand out among your peers. Whatever your job, you must be the best. Your work will serve as evidence that your brand is authentic and that will draw people to you. *Remember, your brand is built on excellence.*

2. **Be politically correct** — Whether it is in the office, on the field, or in school, you must deal with politics. Remain true to who you are in all circumstances. Let your brand shine through and others will follow.

3. **Be in tune with yourself** — Know your strengths and weaknesses in order to utilize them to their fullest. When you change your weaknesses into working positives and build on your strengths, you build a strong brand.

4. **Be focused** — Always keep your end point in mind. We're building a goal mentality, meaning that if you are accomplishing your goals, you'll be moving forward with your purpose and building your legacy. Remember that you have been put on this earth for a reason and your brand is going to help you achieve it. It will also help you to impact the lives of others.

5. **Be present** — It is very important that you are well versed in your field. Never stop learning how to be better and always know the most up-to-date trends so that your brand remains relevant.

When you know what makes you different, your distinctiveness will shine through with confidence. Your strengths help you to elevate your abilities and your corrected weaknesses aid you in crafting a better you. Your unique characteristics assist in the development a one-of-a-kind brand that will stand out against your competition. Understanding your brand is a cornerstone of PCM and successfully transitioning to your next goal.

It's time for you to begin growing your brand. It's a long

process, but a rewarding one if done right. You must remember that building a brand takes time — it will not be accomplished in a few days. It will also take time to maintain and expand your brand, so be patient and ready to create a legacy that will live on forever.

Always remember that you are one-of-a-kind . . .

- ☞ You know yourself better than anyone else.
- ☞ You know your purpose and are heading towards it.
- ☞ You are knowledgeable about your field and career.
- ☞ You are seeing yourself as a brand.
- ☞ You have a brand mindset (aka a *brand-new* mindset).

Chapter

5

A Trusted Brand

"Have a clear idea of who your ideal client/ reader/audience is and position yourself as the expert in that niche. The more specific you can position yourself, the clearer your message will be and the more likely you are to attract your ideal client."

— *Andrea Ayers*

A **personal brand builds trust between you and the** people with whom you engage, so developing it correctly will authenticate who you are, which will increase your network because people will be willing to pay for your product or service. As your network expands so will your opportunities in the form of sales, speaking engagements, jobs, customers, fans, endorsements, and even investments in your company or brand. If you are an athlete, fans trust that you will make the play to win the game; if you are in business, your customers believe that your products are the best in the market, so there is no need to go to the competition. When you win such trust, the people following you will be loyal to you, your product, or your service.

One of the results of creating a trusted brand is the addition of brand ambassadors to help grow and expose you or your business. An ambassador is intended to represent a brand in manner and values. Ambassadors must be able to use their knowledge of the brand to employ promotional tactics that will strengthen the customer-product/service connection and entice others to buy into it as well. Simply put, a brand ambassador is distinguished as a spokesperson designated as an agent to boost product/service sales and create brand awareness.

It goes without saying that ambassadors believe in your product or service, and they will do what is necessary to expand the brand. They will be your word-of-mouth publicity, which sometimes goes further than paid advertising. Apple is a company that relies on brand ambassadors and uses them quite effectively to spread the word about their products and services. Consumers who buy Mac devices spend a lot of money in doing so and will rarely be seen using anything other than a Mac. Brand ambassadors (customers) will wait in line for hours to get the latest addition to their Mac line. They'll know the ins and outs, so they can debate anyone at any time or place regarding the merits of owning an Apple product. Although Apple advertises, they cannot buy word-of-mouth advertising. Imagine if you could have hundreds, thousands, even millions of people shouting from the rooftops about how amazing you are and that there is nothing better than you. A brand ambassador armed with all of the right information can get the word out about you with little to no effort from you or your team.

When a brand ambassador believes in you, they will do anything within reason to see you succeed. They will create blogs for and about you, which will further your message. They will utilize their current social networks to increase your reach among people with whom you may not have connections but are no less your target audience. They will include you in events and charities, giving you more exposure and helping you to give back to the community that supports you. Lastly, brand ambassadors are your mobile fleet — they will wear and carry items with your name, product, or service because they believe in you and what you are doing. Your brand ambassadors could help you move through the PCM process faster than expected by connecting you with the right opportunity or job.

I know you are probably thinking, *Why would anyone want to be my brand ambassador*? Or, *How would I get someone to be my brand ambassador*? Well, your family and friends are your first brand ambassadors. They will be the ones letting the world know about all of your victories at every stage of your life. Athletes gain ambassadors when they excel on the field of play, and those ambassadors could follow them through life if their journey continues on to professional sports or into the corporate world. Employees garner ambassadors when they excel in their field of work. Their superiors and coworkers hold them in high esteem. Call on them whenever their expertise is needed on the job or with outside affiliations.

Lady Gaga has the ultimate brand ambassadors, whom she affectionately calls Little Monsters. As of the beginning of 2014, the Little Monsters have populated her social media accounts to the tune of 3.4 million (Instagram), 41.3 million (Twitter), 6.4 million Likes (Facebook). Her Little Monsters will do anything for her, because they believe she will do anything for them. As a matter of fact, she thanked them with a touching book titled *Heal This Way: A Love Story*, which is composed of letters and quotes accompanying Little Monster portraits. If you want to keep brand ambassadors engaged and working for you, take the time to thank them and show how much you appreciate them.

You want your brand to be known among your sport or industry as the very best so that you'll be profitable (if that's your goal) and valued. As an athlete, a career professional, or an entrepreneur, you aspire to be at the top of your field so that you are recognized and acknowledged for your excellent work above your competitors. That recognition can come in the form of increased press for your brand, business, or position, and can be measured in sponsorships, promotions, and overall profit.

As you continue to move through the PCM process and your brand builds value, it's a *must* that you extend that value to the fans, customers, and people who helped you to build it. Your brand is an extension of the people in your community, the people aspiring to be where you are, those who support you while barely being able to help themselves. We'll discuss giving back in a later chapter, but it should remain a priority to leave a community better than you found it.

Chapter 6

What Does Your Name Say About You?

"Be yourself. Everyone else is already taken.
— *Oscar Wilde*

Your personal brand is constantly being monitored by teachers, fans, potential employers, and customers. After you apply for a job, but before you go in for the interview, your name will be researched online via one of the search engines (Google, Bing, Yahoo, etc.) to see what information can be learned about you. The information discovered might be the reason you are asked, or not asked, for the initial interview. Additionally, if you meet someone and exchange numbers before you go on the first date or attend your first business meeting, you will also be researched online. Based on their findings, these people will form an opinion of you — prior to getting to know the real you. If your online presence is in-line with your actual personality or the person you want them to know, then your brand is fine. If it is not what you want them to know, then you have work to do in order to change online perception.

What is your personal brand saying about you? It's important that you realize your name is your most valuable asset, and unless you change it, it will be with you forever. By determining what you want people to know about you, you'll develop a unique imprint that will make you stand out to employers, schools, customers, and even your next date. You need to be the master of your brand, controlling as much as possible of what people can read or perceive of you. If you do not know how your brand is being perceived, you could be hindering the PCM process.

BRANDERCISE

Online name search. As we discussed earlier, you will be researched online by numerous people and entities, so you should know how you are portrayed on the Internet. Use your favorite search engine to investigate your first and last name — as well as your first, middle, and last name, or any married names — to see what's being said about you.

Did the search reveal what you want people to know about you, or is there some information that you would prefer not be publicized? A very good friend of mine suggested that I meet with a potential client, a former professional athlete who was looking to transition from his current career to his next career. When she forwarded me his résumé, the first thing that I did was a thorough Google search and found some criminal information. I called my friend, questioning why she would refer a prospective client and fail to mention his checkered pass. She was shocked to learn about my findings. Initially, I was going to decline the meeting, but I decided to go because I wanted to know why he had not told anyone about his past. After meeting with him, I discovered that not only were the allegations false, but that he also had a pending court case to get the information deleted from the record. Most importantly, I learned that he never researched himself online and had no idea what was being said about him out there.

Questions to consider when building your personal brand:

1. **Is your fingerprint authentic?** People want to believe in and follow someone or something that is genuine. The people with the most followers are not only the best in their field — making them an authority and someone whom people want to emulate — but they also seem real. They come across as though you're their best friend. People love reality stars because they make everyone feel as if they know them. Your brand has to be as authentic as your fingerprint. Playing a role is a no-no, because in the end you'll lose credibility, fans/customers, or a job.

2. **What do you believe in?** We all believe in something. By this I'm not referring only to religion or politics, but even the smallest or most out-of-the-ordinary things. We all have a core belief system that influences our decision-making.

3. **What is your story?** Everyone relates to stories. If your listener can develop an emotional attachment to your story, you have already won them over and created a brand ambassador. It's amazing how people hold onto a story if it resonates with them, as opposed to facts that coldly demonstrate how important something or someone is. Letting people know your story is an essential part of brand development. How you communicate who you are and what you are doing influences how you are received and the sustainability of your brand. If people can identify with your passion, your history, or anything else about you, an incredible bond emerges.

4. **How will you impact the community?** People want to know how you are going to help make a community a better place. When you excel in your industry you make yourself stand out; in turn, you receive accolades and, hopefully, financial rewards. It's your duty to give back to the people who have supported you as a fan, customer, or employee. By giving back, I do not necessarily mean

financially — you could also give your time mentoring or volunteering.

Honest answers to these questions help to ascertain who you are, what you believe in, and how you will impact those around you. It also helps you to truly utilize the PCM process and make a lasting transition.

Defining your brand doesn't mean creating a persona that is not you. It means highlighting the *you* that you want people to know about, and how you benefit others. It takes deep self-awareness and true answerability. If your brand is a manufactured person, over time people will discover the truth. In the late '80s and early '90s, there was a famous pop duo called Milli Vanilli that amassed international success while earning the coveted GRAMMY® Award for Best New Artist. Unfortunately, their musical career was short-lived, because it was revealed that they did not actually sing on their multi-platinum debut album. This revelation stunned fans around the globe and forever branded them as impostors. They instantly became the butt of jokes and were asked to forfeit their GRAMMY®. Milli Vanilli tarnished their name/reputation and they took a beating from the media and their fans.

The moral of the story: You must develop a personal brand mindset, which means you have to live it, be it, own it, and realize a *brand-new you*. Your personal brand is your unique fingerprint that you need to cultivate and then protect. As we stated previously, your perception of yourself often differs from others' perception of you. In order to determine the general perception of you, you need to ask the right questions of the right people. Start by asking your friends, family, coworkers, and anyone in your life who will give you honest feedback.

BRANDERCISE

How do your friends see you?

Craft a questionnaire to send to friends, family, coworkers, and some of your harshest critics. I suggest sending an email versus having a conversation with them because, as we discussed earlier, when people take the time to write things down they tend to be more specific. Yes, there will be people who will not take your request seriously and will offer vague answers, but that's why you'll send it to 15 to 20 people.

SAMPLE QUESTIONNAIRE

Hello, I'm working on a personal branding exercise and I would appreciate your sincere feedback. Please answer the questions below as best you can:

☞ **List ten words that best describe me?**

☞ **What are my strengths/weaknesses?**

☞ **I could be more successful if I would do, or not do, the following?**

☞ **What is my unique expertise that differentiates me?**

☞ **How do others perceive me personally and/or professionally?**

☞ **What are my goals in life?**

☞ **What do you see me doing in 10 to 15 years?**

After you have gathered information from various sources, compile it. It's time to sit down and take a deep look at all of the feedback. Does the information fall in line with your perception of yourself? Were you surprised about some of the feedback? If all of your information is in line with the perception that you want to portray, great — you can begin to expand on a great foundation. But if it's not, you can begin to strategically combat any negative brand perception and start the process of building the new you. This is an in-depth process, but if you take the time to do it now, you can begin to build the perception you want everyone to have about you. We'll deal with repairing negative information in a later chapter.

Chapter 7

The Pentagon

"Pulling a good network together takes effort, sincerity, and time."

— *Alan Collins*

"**I**t takes a village to raise a child" is a well-known African proverb. It means that although a child's parents may have the primary responsibility of rearing, the child is also being influenced by others with whom he or she comes in contact — teachers, neighbors, church members, etc. It's similar to evolving your personal brand: Although you have developed your current image, skillset, beliefs, and persona, you need a village to help you craft and manage your message. You have already enlisted the help of your friends, family, and community to express how they see you. Next you need the right people to help construct and expand the brand that you want.

Developing your personal brand, and possibly transition-ing to another career or starting a business, is a long, tedious process that can be discouraging if you are not armed with the right knowledge, experience, and people. It's probably in your best interest to find an advisor, coach, or mentor who can give you advice and/or guidance. The terms *advisor*, *coach*, and *mentor* are often used synonymously, but they actually have different meanings. Understanding the meaning of each may help you to choose the right person or people to help you. Depending on your needs, you may be able to get one person to fill all of the roles or you may want separate people for each role. For example, if you are a student trying to decide what industry to pursue or looking for help in an industry you have chosen, all three of these roles may need to be filled.

Advisor, coach, and mentor defined as:

Advisor: An expert in the area or field of interest to you. This person is a great asset when you are conducting research in your chosen industry, because they can either draw upon their experience to give you the necessary information or tell you exactly where to find it. An advisor may or may not have worked in your specific area of interest, but they will definitely be able to supply advice relating to your needs.

Coach: Someone proficient in the methods or procedures necessary to achieve success in your chosen area. Your coach is similar to that of a sporting team — he/she will work with you on a regular basis to help you achieve your specific goals. Coaches will play devil's advocate in order to get you thinking, so that you create a process of your very own. Coaches will want to help you to the extent that one day you won't need them, because you'll have system in place to figure it all out for yourself.

Mentor: Someone who has accomplished goals that you seek to accomplish, and has the knowledge and availability to help you achieve your goals with fewer mistakes and, hopefully, in less time. Although each mentor/mentee relationship is different, mentors usually become available when you need them versus being there the whole time to hold your hand.

You now have a better understanding of some of the people who could help you to develop your personal brand, business, or career. Now it's up to you to pick the right person. First, you need to determine what you really want in the person or people who will guide you. Make a must-have list — a list of qualities/attributes you want in your guide.

Ask yourself questions, such as:

Are you looking for:

- ☞ A male or female?
- ☞ Someone who can connect you with the right people for your interest?
- ☞ Someone who ran a Fortune 500 company or owned a boutique agency?

☞ Someone with specific expertise in social media, international marketing, and/or fundraising?

☞ A person who is not hands-on and will consider your big picture from afar?

Whatever it is, know what you are looking for so you'll know it when you find it.

Begin your search with people you know: friends, family, coworkers, people in associations or organizations to which you belong. They may be able to help you without the learning curve, since they already know you. If you don't know anyone whom you can ask to help you, ask for recommendations or research industry associations and trade magazines, selecting only people who meet your needs and qualifications. After you have made a list of possible candidates, it's time to narrow the search and pick the right one.

1. Interview candidates

Ask each candidate for an informational interview, which could be conducted over the phone, in person at lunch, or maybe over a cup of coffee, depending on your budget. Ask them several questions that will help to ascertain if they're the right person for you. Utilize your list in order to devise the right questions. Keep the meeting brief. Remember, this person is taking time out of their busy schedule to meet with you to see how they could potentially help you. This has to be a good fit for both of you, so it's important that you are ready for their questions, as they will want to know your goals, history, and mindset in order to determine if they would be a good fit to mentor you.

2. Evaluate possible candidates

After your interviews, take time to go over your notes of each candidate and see who fits your requirements best. Contact the candidate and get started right away. You can pick your coach and advisor the same way, if you feel that you need three people to help you with the process. Or maybe one person can serve all three roles. This is an individual decision based on your needs. You actually may find a coach and advisor from your mentor candidate pool.

In order to authenticate your brand you need to bring value not only to yourself, but also to the people who believe in you and your brand. In turn, the people helping you to build your brand need to bring value to it. Singer, songwriter, and performer Anthony Hamilton is a perfectionist at his craft. He demands excellence, and surrounds himself with only the best producers, musicians, and singers to ensure that he is giving his fans a top-notch experience in concert and on recording. I recall being on a promotional tour with him in Philadelphia. We scheduled to meet in the hotel lobby at 9:00 am. Anthony, my radio promotion colleague, and I were waiting for the rest of the band until about 9:30. Before we departed the hotel, Anthony asked my colleague and I if he could have a moment with the band. We obliged and returned 10 minutes later. In our absence, Anthony explained to the band that when they are late it reflects on him, and that is not the message he wants to send. The band understood his desire for excellence, and they were never late again.

Best-selling motivational speaker Jim Rohn said, "You are the average of the five people you spend the most time with." If that statement holds true, then the people you are hanging around are impacting your brand either positively or negatively. Which is it? Make sure that your affiliations are consistent with your message.

After you have defined your brand and core characteristics, build an inner pentagon that mirrors those qualities. A pentagon perfectly embodies the five key people in your life. In addition, if you look at the shape of a pentagon, the points are always directing you in ways to expand who you are. Lastly, a pentagon looks similar to a diamond and the people who are in your pentagon should help to make you the best, turning you from a dirty rock to a special, shiny stone to be admired.

Your pentagon should be strategically constructed with solid people who can help you build your brand and empire. These people need to be likeminded in the sense that they understand where you are and where you want to go. They will be the day-to-day people helping to push you through the PCM process, when you have become stagnant or scared. They will be there when you hit a hurdle and need a little help to get over it. They will hold your hand when you are about to quit and most definitely cheer you on when you have met one of your goals. The great thing about these five people is that they're probably on their own journey to define their brand and build their legacy, so you'll be a part of helping them as well.

Your pentagon may include teammates, coworkers, family, students, or anyone who is a key asset in helping you to achieve your life's goals. These people will become your good friends, always there for you — similar to your mentor, advisor, and/or coach. It's up to you to add or subtract people in your pentagon or your life based upon their value to your brand. I would choose these people similarly to the way you chose your advisor, mentor, and/or coach: Make a list of your needs (marketing background, entrepreneur, etc.), interview, and add to your pentagon. Some people will have a hard time with this, because they might feel as if they're being discarded, but you do not have to erase them from your life — just move them from your Top 5 to your Top 10. They will still be there, but they won't be your go-to people at this time.

PCM uses your network to help push you further. Many of our stars of today met and networked with people who gave them their big break. For instance, Jim Carrey is one of the world's top-paid comedians, but that wasn't always the case. Carrey grew up in Canada, living with his family in a camper van while working eight-hour days at a tire factory to help out. He dropped out of high school and moved to L.A. at the age of 16, where he worked odd jobs to survive. His luck began to change when he started shadowing well-known comedian Rodney Dangerfield at the Comedy Store. It took a while for Carrey to make a name for himself, but he gained favor with Dangerfield and was able to open for him on occasion. This, in turn, opened doors for him, as he started making friends with other comedians, including the Wayans brothers, who gave him his big break on their '90s TV show, *In Living Color*.

Of course, you could argue that Jim Carrey was lucky to have met Dangerfield and hit it off with the Wayans brothers. But his hard work and persistence took him to L.A. in the first place and helped him connect with the right people, who saw value in him and helped him to get to the place where he is today.

The pentagon concept can be used in all parts of your life; it will come up again in Chapter 17, when we discuss how to build a team for your business.

Chapter 8

Creating Your Future

> "Your greatest contribution to helping other people live their destiny is for you to live your own."
>
> — *Alan Cohen*

In building the you that you want others to know about, you need to define your purpose in life and know your *why*. A core principle of PCM is that we were all put on this earth for a reason and that we are all blessed with unique gifts that need to be shared. If we do not share these gifts, we're not only hurting ourselves, but also those who would benefit from them. My grandmother, the matriarch of my family, passed away in 2013 at the young age of 98. I was tasked with writing not only her eulogy, but also her obituary. It was during this process that I began to talk to those who knew her and discovered the impact that she made on the world. My grandmother, Phyllis, was born in Barbados in 1915, the eldest girl of eight children. Although she was a very intelligent woman, she had only an elementary-school education. When she was not cleaning homes and hospitals or looking after children (as a nanny), she spent her life serving others, which is why there were so many stories of people she helped. The following is one such story shared by Patrick G. Forde:

"I first met Sister Beckles 17 years ago, when I started attending Cambridge First Church of the Nazarene. As a fellow Barbadian, it was not long before we formed a unique bond, cemented by weekly conversations about the good old days in Barbados. As our friendship developed, I began to receive weekly "care packages," which basically consisted of a home-cooked meal and a small portion of baked goods. What may have seemed like a simple gesture was a great treasure to me, being a poor student a long way from home.

"However, even after I graduated and began my career, Sister Beckles still brought me my little packages every Sunday after church. This weekly "ritual" continued until about two years ago, when she was well into her nineties. This was not an isolated gesture; Sister Beckles was well known for her culinary skills and her deeds of kindness. She was genuinely concerned about people's well being and willing to do her part to increase their comfort.

"Another aspect of our unique bond was our trips to Barbados. Several years ago, Movita [her daughter, also known as Margot] came up with the idea that her mother and I should be travel companions. So whenever I was planning a trip home, we would book our plane

fares simultaneously. I believe we made three of those pilgrimages over the years. Phyllis was great company and travelled very well despite her advancing years. She was never fazed by any of the inconveniences of modern-day air travel or by such troubles as turbulence. I marveled at her resilience, especially since I myself find air travel boring and unusually gut-wrenching. I kid you not — it did not matter if we were in the middle of a hurricane or the aircraft was flying upside down, she never missed a beat in her conversation. Meanwhile, I would be saying the Lord's Prayer for the umpteenth time and firmly gripping the arm rests.

"One of my lasting memories of her was in August 2005, the day before Hurricane Katrina devastated New Orleans. We were returning from a vacation in Barbados and had picked up an extra travel companion — a young lady who was going to the U.S.A. for the first time to enroll in college. When we reached Miami, the immigration officer informed us that her visa documents were not in order and we would have to sort them out before we could move on. Being the leader of the delegation, I knew I could not leave the young lady by herself in a strange country. So I instructed the airline rep who was assisting us to get Sister Beckles on her connecting flight to Boston, which was leaving in about half an hour. So we parted ways, with me hoping my plan would work. When the visa issue was sorted out,

some three hours later, I proceeded to baggage claim not knowing whether Phyllis had made her flight to Boston. We came down the escalator, and I saw a sight I will never forget. It was late at night and the area was deserted, except for Sister Beckles sitting in a wheel chair surrounded by several baggage handlers who were listening to her as she told them some story or admonished them from the Scriptures. Who knows? All I know is that she had their full attention and had been doing so for a few hours. The queen was on her throne with adoring subjects at her feet, paying homage. Like I said earlier, nothing fazed her.

"I could go on and on. Sister Beckles was many things to many people. You will hear others talk about her as a mother, grandmother, aunt, beloved sister in Christ, prayer warrior, and preacher. For me she was simply a kind friend who I was blessed to know. Now I bid farewell to my travel companion who has gone on her final journey ahead of me."

After hearing other stories like this, I had no problem completing the eulogy and seeing how my grandmother had not only lived her life to the fullest, but had also lived out her purpose. I decided to write my own eulogy, which helped me to discover my purpose, redefine my life, and realize my goals.

BRANDERCISE

Write your eulogy.

What do you want people to say about you when you have passed away? What do you want to be remembered for? Who have you helped along the way? What value did you bring to your business? How did you move your community? How did you treat your friends and people you worked with, and what's your vision for what matters in terms of your personal brand? Write the eulogy that you would want read at your funeral, using the questions above as a guide.

Chapter 9

Purposeful Brand

> "You were put on this earth to achieve your greatest self, to live out your purpose, and to do it courageously."
>
> — *Steve Maraboli*

It's Sunday night and you are already getting the Monday morning blues. You are dreading going to work tomorrow, not because you are not good at what you do or that you don't enjoy it sometimes, but because you feel like there's something more. You can't put your finger on what "more" is, but you know that there has to be "more" to life than this job. At times you have considered pursuing other things, but then you received a bonus at work for a job well done or you were rewarded with a promotion that you were not expecting, which pushed back the need to find out what you really should be doing. Stop putting off the inevitable and take some time to find out why you were put on this earth.

I'm sure you know someone who has known what they were supposed to do from the time they started walking. Sheryl Swoopes knew from a young age that she wanted to play basketball, and her determination to succeed earned her the honor of being the first player signed to the WNBA. She is often called the Female Michael Jordan due to her incredible skills. Her legacy has been solidified by the following accolades: three Olympic gold medals, three WNBA MVP Awards, and a Nike shoe named after her (she's the first woman to have that honor). Sheryl has lived her destiny and now, as head coach of the women's basketball team at Loyola University Chicago, she's helping others live theirs. We all wish that it could come to us that easily, but most of us stumble through life before we discover exactly why we were put here, and then we grow angry — because if we had found out earlier, we could've been living a happy life and positively impacting the lives of others.

By not living our purpose we are not only hurting ourselves, but we are also hurting those who are negatively impacted by us not fulfilling our potential. It's essential to pursue what you love, so that you can wake up every morning excited about your day and what you are going to accomplish. Here's the most exciting part: Your work will not feel laborious. Imagine if you could use your innate strengths to do something you love, whether it be at a 9-to-5 or your own company. Right now you may have a hobby that you pursue in your downtime (hopefully you're getting paid for it), but if you could transform your passion into a full-time opportunity, it could be the answer to your dreams.

Like the PCM process, finding your life's purpose is typically not something accomplished overnight. You first have to take time to delve deep into your inner self and be open to listening to whatever you may find. It can be a daunting journey, but also a rewarding one if you not only find your purpose, but also live it proudly. Your purpose could be the missing link to something that will allow you to make a mark on this world. It's important that you understand that your purpose doesn't have to be curing cancer; it has to be *your purpose*, and if it helps one person, then it was worth discovering. By helping one person, you might just change the world.

BRANDERCISE

Find your purpose.

Your life's purpose is like a guide to help increase your chances of experiencing as much happiness, success, and fulfillment as you can for the rest of your life. Please note that there are no guarantees in life, so defining your purpose doesn't mean that everything will, all of a sudden, be perfect. Life will always be a work-in-progress this is just helping to direct you.

---

1. Discover your passion(s).

What do you love to do? Make a list of all the things you *love* to do. Close your eyes and imagine if you had no responsibilities, what would make you happy to wake up and do every day? Ask yourself, *If I could monetize an action, what would that action be*? Remember, no limits!

2. Unearthing your talents

It's time to take a deep look at yourself to determine the things you do well naturally. Initially, this list may stump you, because it can be difficult to look at your day-to-day activities and determine what you are good at. You have been trained to look only at the things you do at work, at school, or on the field. Unfortunately, your current situation may not be a good indicator of what you do well. Oftentimes your job is a source of income, not a lifetime occupation. Your athletic ability is only one of your many talents. It may not even be your primary talent, but rather the thing that comes easily to you. By "lifetime occupation," I mean an occupation that encompasses all of your assets, an occupation that you are excited to do every day, an occupation for which you have trained and continue to receive education to expand your knowledge. You must explore all avenues in your life to discover all of your talents. This list might include things such as mentoring to teens, organizing the homes of hoarders, set design, jingle writing, gourmet cooking, etc. It's essential that you enlist the help of family, friends, coworkers, and advisors, because they may see things in you that you have not considered.

3.   Compile a kudos list

What thing(s) do you do for which you always receive rave reviews? It's time to think back to all of those heartfelt, "warm and fuzzy" compliments. What are people always patting you on the back for? Cooking? Singing? Organizing? Painting? Yard work? Take your time. The list you have compiled thus far consists of what you think of you, but now it's time to pull out some of those emails, cards, or notes people sent to thank or compliment you for work well done, or just for being a good friend.

We often forget the good things people say, but we always seem to remember the bad things or the things we have done wrong. By the end of this exercise you should be smiling.

4.   Be honest about your dislikes

Compile a list of things you dislike doing. Go through your list of talents and kudos, crossing out all of the things that you do well, but don't like to do. There may be things you currently do at work, home, church, and/ or school. We all have something, even if we don't want to admit it. Secondly, make a list of other jobs/duties you dislike doing. This is kind of abstract, but it will help you to learn about yourself.

5. Examine your downtime

What do you enjoy doing in your me-time? Develop a list of me-time activities. This could be a key indicator of your purpose; many times the things we spend our time doing, dreaming, or talking about are the things we're meant to do.

6. Never stop learning

What kinds of things pique your interest? Write down the types of things you like to read, the literature that draws and holds your attention. Start with your favorite books, magazines, or blogs, and then make it more specific. Write down the industries and/or types of books (i.e. sports, business, fashion, music, self-help, fitness, education).

This process was created to help you begin looking more deeply within yourself and to aid you in realizing what you should and shouldn't be doing. If you truly open yourself to the possibility of doing something you love verses doing something to pay the bills, you may find your purpose and begin living it. If you take these lists to heart you'll begin to see a pattern of things you should be doing. You'll feel an emotional pull to certain items, and you should thoroughly explore how you might pursue these things full-time. Are they part of an already-established job within a company or are they the building blocks of a company (profit or nonprofit) that you should start? If there are things that you can put into action right away, like writing or art, begin doing a little bit every day. Start writing your own blog, be a guest writer on someone else's blog, or just begin journaling. Start small and then think how you might do it full-time. It just might get you to thinking about writing your own book.

Chapter 10

What Is Your Motive?

"He who has a why to live for can bear almost any how."

— *Friedrich Nietzsche*

What makes you get up every morning to go to work? Is it simply that you have to put food on the table or pay your rent/mortgage? If that's the case, are you living or merely surviving? What's your *why*, and by that I mean what's your motive? Your *why* is the reason you wake up in the morning happy and excited to do what you were put on this earth to do. We should all have a *why* for our life, because it makes the hard times bearable. During the PCM process there will always be unforeseen obstacles as you try to achieve your goals, but imagine if you have a secret source of purpose that pushes you through to the end, helping you to overcome, evade, or convert them.

My *why* came about via a TED Talk on YouTube. A friend suggested I watch the video, and while it took me some time to do so, I finally saw it: Simon Sinek discussing "how great leaders inspire action." According to Sinek, "People do not buy what you do. They buy why you do it." He further clarified that the goal is not to sell to people what you have; the goal is to connect with people who believe what you believe. After watching this video I yelled at my computer, "Simon, this is exactly what I've been talking about regarding building a brand!"

If you create an authentic brand, letting people know why you do what you do, they will not only believe in you, but they will also buy into your dream. What made this video so amazing for me is that this is not just a theory developed by Sinek — it's actually a proven fact based on the study of the human brain by scientists. He highlights the fact that the brain is made up of three parts, two of which help us to make decisions based on emotion. The third part makes decisions based on fact. If Sinek is correct in his assumption that people do not buy what we do, but why we do it, then they are making their decisions based upon emotion.

I've been teaching this to friends, family, and clients for years, but I never stated it in such a succinct and eloquent way. Sinek's theory hit me like a ton of bricks: *How can you expect anyone to believe in you or follow you if you don't know why you do something*? Many of us unhappily go to a job every day just to collect a paycheck and benefits, never stopping to think about why we do what we do and, more importantly, whether we're doing what we were put on this earth to do. We seem to find it easy to settle. But there's so much more to life than that. Shouldn't we want to be fulfilled by what drives us? What makes us happy to wake up every day and do what God put us on this earth to do?

What Is Your Motive? _____

While Sinek's video made things crystal clear to me, it was not until I discovered my *why* that my life really changed. You are probably wondering, *What is her* why? *Why does she get up in the morning to do what she does*? *What gets her excited*? Well, my *why* is my love for watching people's faces light up when they talk about *their* passions. One night a friend of mine came over for dinner and we talked for hours about his non-profit. This guy is really laid-back and rarely gets excited, but this one night, as he described how he wanted to help the people in a city where he lived for a short while, a smile crossed

Serena Williams will be remembered as one of the greatest tennis players in history. She has been playing since the age of four and has amassed 32 major titles over the course of her career. She first used her father's "you are the best and no one can tell you different or prove different" attitude to help her overcome and achieve. As she got older, dealing with racism, health issues, negative talk, and other obstacles, her *why* changed. She stated, "I'm not doing anything for money. I'm doing it because I love it. Anyone who knows me knows that I have a simple life and enjoy the simple pleasures of being happy and making people happy. That's really what this is all about." And she's right — if you can find something that makes you happy and you wake up every day excited to do it, whether you are getting paid or not, you have not only found your *why*, but also your purpose.

his face and stayed there. You could see his eyes glow as he saw himself helping kids see a different future. His passion was oozing from every pore, so much so that I could almost see his vision. When someone knows their *why*, you can live their dreams with them. By the end of the night I was smiling just as much as he was, because I understood his *why* and his passion. There's nothing like that feeling. I help people because I love to see their breakthrough. My *why* is already unlocking doors for me and I hope that, if you haven't already, you will determine your *why* and unlock the door to your future.

BRANDERCISE

Defining your *why*? What makes you do the things you love to do? What makes you pursue your passion? What are you most passionate about? How is your business, career, or school associated with your passion? What does success mean to you? If you could make a difference to anyone or anything, what would it be? Answering the questions above will help you to crystalize your *why*.

Chapter 11

Crafting Your Brand

> "All of us need to understand the importance of branding. We are CEOs of our own companies: Me Inc. To be in business today, our most important job is to be head marketer for the brand called You."
>
> — *Tom Peters*

Are you ready? Grab a pencil, because you are going to begin sketching the exact image you want to see when looking in the mirror. You may not be an artist, but you know exactly who you are and how you want others to view you. Now it's time to find the artist in you and sketch the perfect image of yourself. The piece of paper you are about to use is not clean, because by the time you are in high school your brand is already being formulated, and as you go through college and/or your chosen profession you continue to add to the portrait. The great thing about your pencil is that it has an eraser, so you are able to go back, remove some of the perceptions formed over the years, and redraw the perfect image you want the world to see. But how do you actually make that happen?

Your reputation is a key part of building your personal brand and successfully navigating the PCM process. In order to rise to the top of your class, industry, or profession, you need to be an expert. You need to be the one the teacher calls upon when he/she has a prospective assignment or internship, the company chooses when they want to impress a client, or the team picks on draft day. Ask yourself, *How would I like potential coaches, schools, clients, or companies to think of me*? Your brand should embody your purpose (why you were put on this earth), your *why* (what motivates you), your values (core beliefs), and your goals (eulogy). You should be the best at whatever you do. Your actions of excellence will tell your brand story for you without you having to do the work.

In clutch situations, when the New England Patriots are trailing, Tom Brady will almost always spark a highlight-reel play that carries them to victory. Coaches, head office staff, and fans don't worry when Brady has the ball in his hands, because they know he'll make something happen. The surprise comes only when he *doesn't* live up to his name — i.e. his brand. Brady didn't develop his brand by talking about what he does on the field via social media or billboards; he let his actions on the field build his brand, while using social media and the press only to showcase the personal side of his life — the things he does off of the field. This gives his fans (possible brand ambassadors) a complete picture of him. You are about to develop a written version of your brand, which is actually an accumulation of your actions. What's the old saying? "Actions speak louder than words." Make your actions draw the pictures that your words have written.

A personal mission statement is the first step to developing your story, because it makes you succinctly articulate the purpose of your life, your goals, your beliefs, and how you'll utilize them. A personal statement is a verbal declaration of who you are and what you want to do, based on your values, beliefs, and goals. It's a work-in-progress statement for you to read and review, to keep you focused and on target with your goals and purpose. It's also the foundation of all of the other branding tools and documents you'll use to develop your . . . legacy.

Creating a personal mission statement is not a quick process, as you need to take a look within yourself to express, concisely, your deepest beliefs and ambitions. You need to take some time to determine all aspects of this statement, because when people read it they're reading the essence/soul of you. If crafted correctly, this statement will inscribe your pathway in your mind so that it becomes a part of you, rather than something you think about occasionally.

A mission statement is not long; it is a phrase or a few sentences that describe your goals, purpose, and the general ideas of your personal brand. So, let's create a personal mission statement.

Below are a couple examples of personal mission statements:

AMANDA STEINBERG — FOUNDER, DAILYWORTH.COM

"To use my gifts of intelligence, charisma, and serial optimism to cultivate the self-worth and net-worth of women around the world."

Steinberg launched *Daily Worth* in 2009 to help women build wealth. Since then, she's grown her site to more than one million subscribers. "I believe financially empowered women are the key to world peace," she told Stephanie Vozza of *Fast Company*.

DENISE MORRISON — CEO, CAMPBELL SOUP COMPANY

"To serve as a leader, live a balanced life, and apply ethical principles to make a significant difference."

As Morrison told journalist Stephanie Vozza, "The personal mission statement was important for me because I believe that you can't lead others unless you have a strong sense of who you are and what you stand for. For me, living a balanced life means nurturing the academic, physical, and spiritual aspects of my life so I can maintain a sense of well-being and self-esteem."

BRANDERCISE

Craft your very own personal mission statement:

Combine the key elements of your eulogy, purpose, *why*, and passion. Your eulogy highlights all of the successful things you have accomplished in your life and how you impacted those in your community. Your purpose is the reason you were put on this earth. Your *why* is what motivates you not only to excel, but also to live your purpose. Together, these statements are you. They are your personal brand.

1. Craft it: *Reread your eulogy and then summarize it in four sentences. I know you are thinking, This is my life you're talking about. How can I cut it down to just four sentences? I understand your hesitancy and I know it will be hard, especially since you have impacted tons of lives and accomplished all of your life's goals (or at least your eulogy states that you have). This first draft will be long, but that's OK — this is a work-in-progress. When writing your mission statement think about these questions: How will you fulfill your purpose? What is your why? What personal* *and professional roles will you hold? How will you impact the lives of others? What are your goals? What are your beliefs?*

2. Refine it: *Edit and rewrite it until you have concise statement, so that anyone who reads it can easily understand who you are at the core.*

3. Get feedback: *Send your statement-in-progress to your pentagon partners, coach, advisor, mentor, and anyone who's knowledgeable about what you are doing, and ask them what they think your personal brand statement means. Also, send it to those who are not familiar with your long-term plans and see if they get a clear understanding of your brand. If your mission statement is on target, then tweak it a bit where necessary and print it or put it somewhere you can see it on a regular basis. If, on the other hand, people are unable to articulate your brand the way it's intended, then you may have to start over and refine it so that it's easier to understand. You want your brand ambassadors and those working* *for you to clearly understand your personal statement so that they can help spread your vision.*

4. Evolve: *As your personal brand evolves, so should your statement, as it is a continuous work-in-progress. However, if crafted perfectly the first time you write it, it may never change.*

If you took the time to develop your personal mission statement, you have a greater self-awareness — a tool you can use to communicate your intentions to the world, as well as a foundation for a plan to build your legacy and complete the PCM process. Here are two other tools that you can develop from your mission statement: a brand tagline and brand mantra.

Brand Promise vs. Brand Tagline

Is "Just Do It" Nike's brand promise or brand tagline? If you said "brand tagline," you are correct. Nike's brand mantra is "Authentic Athletic Performance," which was developed by brand pioneer Scott Bedbury. "Just Do It" is a tagline for a promotional campaign that has changed several times over the years. Although a brand mantra — or, as I like to call it, brand promise — can change as a brand changes, it typically doesn't, especially if it's something that resonates with the people using it. I use the term *brand promise* because I believe that, when crafted correctly, it provides the assurance that one will accomplish something specific or that a particular action will have an intended outcome.

"Just Do It" versus "Authentic Athletic Performance" shows the key difference between a brand tagline and a brand promise. In his best-selling book, *Building Measuring and Managing Brand Equity*, Kevin Lane Keller describes Nike's brand promise thusly: "Nike's brand mantra put a particular emphasis on maintaining authenticity, by which we also meant integrity and purity, front and center . . . All products and activities associated with Nike likewise had to be athletic, not leisurely . . . Finally, every Nike product had to exude world-class performance and meet the demands of the world's finest athletes, even though such athletes represented a microscopic piece of Nike's total business . . . 'Authentic Athletic Performance' was a simple idea, but like so many simple ideas, its execution and implementation could be complex, not to mention challenging, daunting, and even painful, when it came down to forgoing revenue-generating activities because they violated these accepted core values." Your brand promise should incorporate many layers, so that it can be a timeless promise evolving over the lifespan of the brand.

From the above description, you can see that Nike has stayed true to their brand promise through all of their taglines. Brand promise is more of an internal phrase typically used by those working for the brand to build it and create a cohesive campaign, which will include several crafty taglines over the long haul. A tagline can be seen as more of the external-facing element of the brand — a concise statement used to position it. A brand promise isn't just a brand builder; it is its very life-blood, which employees will use as a bible . . . if they're not using the mission statement.

What is a brand promise? It's a phrase that helps you to identify with a person/company. It helps everyone involved in building the brand stay consistent throughout everything that's created or used in conjunction with the brand. When developing such a promise it's important to showcase the brand's beliefs, vision, and core competencies, which you should be able to ascertain from the mission statement.

A great brand promise should:

☞ **Be simple and clear.**

Everyone reading it should be able to ascertain the brand purpose without much explanation. In other words, it's precise, creative, and descriptive.

☞ **Be stimulating and motivating.**

The brand promise is something that's used mostly internally to help position the brand, so it must evoke an emotion that will help to place it in the best light possible.

☞ Be memorable.

This promise needs to stand out in a crowded field of competition and be remembered by all who heard it, not because it's simple and clear, but because it represents all of the brand's attributes.

☞ Stay timeless.

Be able to represent the brand now and in the future. A brand promise comes from your mission statement, which encompasses where you came from, where you are, and especially where you are headed.

☞ Be concise.

The promise is usually three to six words summarizing everything about the brand. Remember, it's your guide to building a cohesive brand and will answer some of the following questions:

- ✔ Who am I?
- ✔ What are my core values?
- ✔ What do I want to be known for — now and in the future?

Chapter 12

Branded Image

> "Your name and face carry your brand in both reality and virtual reality, such that wherever they are cited, your personal brand is at stake."
>
> — *Dan Schawbel*

You only have one chance to make a great first impression, so make sure your brand correctly tells your story the first time — and that includes images in the physical and/or digital world. It takes only a glance to evaluate you based solely on your appearance. In some instances, people may begin assessing you based on the way you stand, speak, and behave. It may not be ethically right, but it's socially accepted that you will be judged by your looks when you're met in person or seen online. It's second nature or due diligence (if you're a hiring manager/coach) to research a person before a meeting or interview, to find out more about them. This first encounter (whether in person or online) is crucial, because it may determine if you are able to continue to the next step of the process.

We always think of the first impression when discussing employment or dating. But it pertains to teams, clients, or other organizations — no matter the entity, you are being judged from the moment you are seen. Think of yourself as the perfect gift: The first thing people see is the wrapping, which could make them want to rush to open the box or just leave it there until another time. They will not know what the gift is until they take off the bow, ribbon, wrapping paper, open the box, and pull back the tissue paper. The gem inside remains hidden until they peel away at all of the pretty things covering it up. Conversely, if the wrapping is beautiful, but there's nothing inside, you will want to discard it, and not dig deeper to see if there is something worthwhile hiding — as it pertains to you, it simply means that you need to work on the inner you.

Is your image telling the same story as your written brand (mission statement)? If not, it's time to bring your vision to reality with image branding. There are two types of personal image branding: your reflection in the mirror (a big part of your brand is what people see) and branding collateral or marketing material (logo, business cards, and website). It's essential that the image you are showing to the world be inline with everything that you have developed.

As you craft your brand, cultivate an appearance that mirrors the goals you are trying to accomplish. Your brand will excel when you begin to ensure that the outward appearance mirrors the inner self. Dress for the job you want, not the job that you have. In essence, if you want to be a lawyer start looking the part, and although we have different views of what a lawyer may look like, you have to dress how *you* think a lawyer dresses. Ensure that your business cards, website, and all other image branding pieces reflect what you want and where you are going.

Tattoo(s)

Express yourself with ink if it helps to tell the story of your brand. It's been noted that over 30% of millennials have branded their bodies with at least one tattoo. Expressing yourself via body ink or even piecing might be your thing; however, it's worth noting that many companies have hiring managers from a generation that may not understand or appreciate body branding. Until you decide if you are going to have a corporate career or not, limit your tattoos to places that can be concealed by work clothes. If you find a workplace that's more liberal, be creative and put your piercings wherever you choose.

In 2001 Benjamin Amos was hired to work at a Starbucks in Dallas, TX. At the time, he had various tattoos, which were never questioned by management. He worked his way up to shift manager and, according to him, no one commented about his tattoos. All that time, he complied with Starbucks rules and kept them hidden from plain view. Until 2008, that is, when he was fired by the store manager, because the regional and district manager didn't like the tattoos. While his direct manager called him a week later to rehire him, Amos filed a lawsuit, stating that female employees were not fired for their tattoos. This is an example of being treated poorly by self-expression via tattoos, but you could experience this same discrimination from people not understanding your brand or your ink.

Hair

Feel free to express your brand through your hair. Fans, employers, and society as a whole have an opinion regarding accepted hairstyles for certain careers. But it's important that you be yourself and do what you think is best for your brand. Most employers will be comfortable with whatever you feel comfortable with. But of course, there are some exceptions to the rule. Before you enter an industry or go on a job interview, make sure you research the company's rules and know the environment in which you'll be working in order to style your hair accordingly. You also have to realize that no matter what you do, some people will simply not like your hairstyle. You could be the best candidate for the job, doing amazing things in the community, or have the cure for cancer, but if your hair does not meet someone's standards you may be ostracized or not taken seriously. Some experts say you should cater your hairstyle to the general office style but still be you . . . What does that mean? If you are comfortable with purple hair and you show up at a conservative law firm for an interview, you may not be given the opportunity to prove your skills. It's not right, but society is still learning that different doesn't mean unqualified. It just means your brand is unique, but it does not determine your ability to do the job. It's probably surprising to learn that in many non-traditional jobs there's little to no leeway on unique hairstyles.

In the 2012 Summer Olympics, United States gymnast Gabby Douglas received criticism for her hair, which was pushed back with pins like the other gymnasts' — the only difference being that she had a visible weave. People felt that her that hair was "unkempt." One tweet asked, "Why hasn't anyone tried to fix Gabby's hair?" Another read, "Gabby Douglas gotta do something with this hair. These clips and brown gel residue ain't it." Gabby was excelling at her job, carving out her place in history, yet the public was fixated on her hair. It's a shame, because worrying about Gabby's hair made many people not experience her full performance, which resulted in not one, but two gold medals. Remember, you'll always have critics, but you need to be comfortable with who you are and what you look like. Let your skillset speak for you and the world will accept your appearance. Take a page from America's sweetheart, Gabby Douglas.

Collateral

Your brand appearance deals not only with your physical attributes, but also the items you design to let the world know of and about you. These include your logo, website, social media, and other marketing materials. Collateral branding is the assemblage of marketing materials used to promote your message. It's the tangible evidence of the brand that expresses its core beliefs and strengths. It plays a key role in helping you reach your target audience and relaying your message directly to them in their language.

What do I mean by *language*? Well, every one of us is attracted to, comprehends, and retains images and information differently. That said, it is important when you are considering creating your collateral that it speaks to your core audience. Clear, concise, and specific collateral branding propels your vision from the your business cards, website, and social media to the right audience. Use your collateral and online presence to extend your brand image.

An essential part of collateral branding is logo design — it's what reminds your target audience of your personal brand. Make sure that it's clearly represented on your business cards, presentations, and digital profiles. Your logo may be your name or a moniker that defines you. In creating your logo, it's best to find a graphic designer whom you trust. Get recommendations and make sure to check out their work, so you know that they're in sync with the type of image you want to create. In order to develop the best logo for your brand, you should've crafted your mission statement, defined your purpose, and figured out your *why* . . . Your designer needs to understand a few essentials about your brand before they can begin creating your unique logo.

In an effort to get the best logo, you need to make sure that your graphic designer is aware of your defining characteristics/beliefs and what differentiates you from the competition. In most cases, your designer will give you a few choices. Spend time with them. Show them to your mentor/advisor/coach and trusted pentagon to get their thoughts. Make sure that you check the color, font, size, and orientation. Ask the designer to make changes until you are happy with final product. Initially, this process will be a lot of fun and a little daunting, but when you pick the *one* — the perfect logo — you'll be bursting with excitement about your personal brand. What are some quick and easy tools to build your personal Brand?

- ✔ Business cards
- ✔ PowerPoint portfolio of your skills
- ✔ Email address
- ✔ Letterhead
- ✔ Brochures
- ✔ Envelopes
- ✔ Banners (physical and virtual)
- ✔ Postcards

Website

Build your online presence by creating a digital portfolio that expresses who you are, both personally and professionally, from content to design. There are two ways to do this: Hire a Web designer to devise a site for you or use one of the easy, new personal branding websites. If you have a Web designer create a website or blog for you, then you'll need to reserve a domain name. This is the name that people will type in the search bar to learn more about you. In most cases this will be your name, but it may alternately be a nickname or phrase that represents you. You can go on sites like godaddy.com or networksolutions.com to see what URLs are available. If your name is not available, investigate similar options. Be innovative, but not cheesy and clichéd.

Your domain should be identical to your brand name. It's important that your URL be short, simple, and easy to remember. It should not need explanation or be difficult to spell. Just like choosing your logo or deciding on your brand name, the process of choosing a URL should be strategic. You want a memorable, timeless URL that will help to define your brand. Side note: If you have children, reserve their names as well (you can never start branding too early).

Your website or blog will allow you to have a personal email address and give you a forum that showcases your brand (i.e. your appearance, skillset, interests, and beliefs). Make sure you incorporate your new logo if you developed one for your brand. If you choose the second option — to use a free, do-it-yourself branding website, such as Wix, Brandyourself.com, Strikingly.com, or About.me — you will also receive some added features, including SEO (Search Engine Optimization). Such do-it-yourself sites are terrific for quickly and efficiently building your brand. You can hire a web designer to come in and fine-tune your website, after you have developed your brand and have acquired additional capital.

Social media/online content

Ensure that your online profiles expose your brand clearly and concisely, so that the perception is in-line with the actual brand. See that all of the information you put on the site is up-to-date and in sync with your brand. Although the Web is a great asset with which to build your message, remember that everything you craft and share is open to advice, criticism, and feedback. Popular social media sites are good to start building your brand, although it's not necessary to be on all of them. Start with one, master it, and then move on to the next. A few of the popular sites worth trying are listed below, but new ones are always popping up, so choose a site and make sure you are catering to your style and audience.

- ✔ LinkedIn
- ✔ Google+
- ✔ Instagram
- ✔ Facebook
- ✔ Twitter
- ✔ YouTube
- ✔ Pinterest
- ✔ Vine

Remember that a fan, client, or employee may connect with your brand for the first time online, so make sure that it represents you well. All of your online profiles (social media or websites) are part of your brand and public image, so they must represent the authentic you. In most cases you will not be there personally to help them understand you, so your online presence must be perfectly constructed. Do you know that everything you do on the Internet is archived? Yes, *everything* that you write or post online is available for the world to see at any time. Use the Internet to enhance your strategy by writing appropriate content or posting brand-relevant images.

When you are building your brand you should use the Internet to enhance your strategy by only writing or posting images of things you hope to aid in your development. I suggest that you keep your personal life private. Airing the ups and downs of your personal relationships may be entertaining to some, but it's not helping your brand, so it's smart to avoid doing it. Additionally, I know it's tempting to be vocal about certain topics your friends are discussing, but if it's not benefiting your brand, say nothing on social media and save it for a one-on-one conversation. By being aware of what you post, you're better able to prevent the loss of a valuable opportunity, job, or brand ambassador.

Tweets, Facebook posts, and any other websites where you have posted negative comments about a race, sex, or religion can make you lose a job, get kicked off a team, or suspended from a school. Do you recall Justine Sacco, former IAC PR director who posted the following tweet before boarding a flight to South Africa: "Going to Africa. Hope I don't get AIDS. Just kidding. I'm white"? Before she landed, her tweet went viral and she was immediately labeled a racist. The tweet and its fallout cost her a job. If that was not bad enough, whenever her name is searched on the Internet, the incident is the first thing that comes up. The craziest thing is that, per reports of people who know her, the tweets don't represent who she really is. Sacco was born in South Africa and raised in the U.S., but her father was actually raised in South Africa. Everyone who knew her said she's far from a bigot, but she's now branded as one and has to do some serious brand management to correct that perception.

When your collateral and online platforms are working cohesively, they become your core *personal* message, exclusive to you — branding you. As you continue to grow and expose your brand, you're responsible for how it's presented, but you're also responsible for living the brand you are creating. Your brand will constantly evolve based on various developments and improvements.

BRANDERCISE

Create an online profile.

Either hire a Web designer or use one of the do-it-yourself sites, such as strikingly.com, which uses your LinkedIn profile to create a personal website for you. You can also develop your website on Brandyourself. com or Wix.com, in a few short steps. All of these websites have a SEO feature as a bonus to help you market your website.

Chapter 13

Begin the Conversation

> "To effectively communicate, we must realize that we are all different in the way we perceive the world and use this understanding as a guide to our communication with others."
>
> — *Tony Robbins*

It's time to tell everyone who you are and how your brand is going to help them. You have constructed your perfect message, but unless you effectively communicate it, all of your hard work will go to waste. Where do you begin? Where do you tell your story in a way that will connect you with the right people? Before you can decide how you are going to communicate or precisely what you are going to say, you'll have to determine "the right people," also known as your target market. Based on that market, your resources will determine how you'll engage with them and the types of messages you'll be using.

A target market is a group of people who have similar beliefs, interests, or history. It focuses marketing energy on a person or brand in order to increase awareness or sales. If you are a graphic designer working at a company, your audience may include your boss, any creative departments, and/or select upper management. Outside of your work environment, your audience might be those companies or people who cater to your design aesthetic. If your focus is logos, you could cater to anyone looking to develop their brand, companies seeking to rebrand, authors, entertainers, athletes, even entrepreneurs, to name just a few. As an athlete trying to get on a team, your target market is all of the decision makers, but if you're an athlete trying to transition out of the sport, your target market includes those who can impact your new business or occupation.

If you do not define your target market and, instead, make the novice mistake of marketing to everyone, you will end up marketing to *no one*. Many people who do not understand the concept of target marketing feel that if they don't market to everyone, then they will be limiting themselves and missing out on possible prospects. If you market to everyone, and the people who come across your brand have nothing in common with you, it does nothing for your brand. Instead, if you do your research and determine who will buy/sell your product or who will benefit from it, then you will have an avid listener. The people who come in contact with your brand will evaluate it and determine if it's a good fit for them based on things they admire about it. If they like it, you may acquire ambassadors who will help to expand its presence or an opportunity to take your business to another level.

Find your target market by determining your ideal client/ customer, or the company for which you would love to work. These targets need to be defined as much as possible, so that you can devise a plan to get your brand in front of them. If you're a student trying to get your first corporate job, or if you're seeking employment at an up-and-coming company within your industry, ask yourself the following questions: *What companies are highly regarded within my industry? What companies align with my core beliefs? What companies have a work environment in which I would thrive?* Make a list and then narrow it down to a manageable number that will allow you to research the specific department in which you see yourself working every day. Try to learn about the people within the department. As an entrepreneur, you should go through the same drill to determine your ultimate target audience and then create a plan to reach them.

How, exactly, do you reach this awesome group of people who will help to expand your brand? Your website, blog, and social media sites are a great start for your online marketing plan, but you should also connect with your audience physically — at networking events, conferences, seminars, or wherever else they might patronize. Conduct a little research to see which marketing outlet(s) your target market responds to. Do they talk on Facebook, Twitter, or Google+? Do they read blogs, websites, and industry posts on LinkedIn? Maybe they still believe in connecting with people in person at Lunch & Learns, networking events, or conferences. Whatever their mode of communication, you must find it and meet them there.

In order to communicate effectively you must fine-tune your observations of how your brand is being received, how you are affecting that reception, and to whom your brand is being delivered. To maintain strong messaging you must have a strong identity. Choose carefully the outlets you use to communicate your brand to the world. If your demographic is 70-plus and they are not on Instagram or Pinterest, then those two sites are not where you need to focus your efforts, because you would be wasting time and missing crucial ambassadors. Choose the right communication method for your demographic and make sure that you or your team are utilizing it to its fullest.

Defining your audience, locating them, and crafting the correct message are all key components in telling the world about your brand. Now the fun part begins: Engage, engage, engage. Start the conversation by telling the world about *you* . . . what you do, how you do it, and most importantly why you do what you do. Effectively working through the PCM process demands that you always be consistent in communicating your brand.

Online presence

Social media is a great place to reconnect with childhood friends, meet new business partners, and seek opportunities not directly available to you. It's an even better place to launch your brand. Most people use Facebook, Twitter, Instagram, Google+, or Pinterest to communicate what's going on in their daily lives. When you start using social media and your very own website to communicate your mission statement, purpose, and brand promise, you are crafting a message about yourself, which begins the process of setting you apart from your competition.

If you wisely craft your brand messages, you can use social media to build a huge platform. However, if you use social media inappropriately you'll hurt your brand — and *correcting* it is much more difficult than *crafting it*. Remember, your social media engagement is a bird's-eye view of your brand, so utilize it with a clear goal in mind. Your interactions on social media develop your brand and construct your reputation. Choose content (words and pictures) that will enhance your brand. Posting pictures that include you and illegal substances, or sexually explicit content, can prevent you from playing on a professional team or getting a job.

In 2012, Yuri Wright, a highly recruited cornerback at Bosco Prep High School in Ramsey, NJ, was expelled from school for tweeting sexually explicit and racial content. He was discussing things that many teenage boys talk about in the locker room, but he made the fatal mistake of making his thoughts public. Though such statements should not be made anywhere, they should most definitely not be made via social media. Yuri's inexperience regarding social media cost him a scholarship to the school of his dreams, the University of Michigan, which has adopted a zero-tolerance policy toward such social media antics.

In March 2014, I attended the Atlanta Business Chronicle — Business on Sports Summit, where Atlanta Braves GM Frank

Wren stated that before he signed Ervin Santana, he checked out his social media profiles to see what he was posting and whom he was following. In the end, the Braves signed Santana, but this process is yet another example that talent is no longer the only thing being considered in sports deals.

Another factor that people don't seem to take into consideration when starting up their social media pages: the people who follow/friend you help to define your brand. If the people in your pentagon have views or opinions that are contrary to your message, they could harm it and you'll have to engage in damage control to fix it. For instance, a friend's friend on Facebook posted a video containing very explicit material that appeared on my timeline. As a result, I deleted my friend, because that was not the content/message for which I wanted to be known.

Remember, what's posted online *stays* online. It's a permanent record.

On the job, on the field, in the classroom

Your personal brand is your reputation as an employee, entrepreneur, athlete, or student, so you need to be the best in order to stand out in your specific arena. We have already discussed the fact that your brand gets you through doors or keeps you out of them, so the best way to communicate within your chosen field is to excel. If you are the answer to what they need, they will always see value in you, promote you, and pick you for various opportunities.

Public speaking

If you become the expert in your field, speaking is the perfect opportunity to make the world aware of who you are and what you know. Panels are a great place to highlight your knowledge while giving you a platform to showcase your brand. Speaking can also be an additional source of income. You might actually like it enough to make a career out of it. What better way to further your cause or expand your brand than to become a professional speaker?

Résumé/PowerPoint

Your résumé should offer the same professional snapshot as your mission statement, based upon the current status of your career. I know you are probably saying, "Well, I'm in school and I haven't worked anywhere yet." Have you completed an internship or performed community service in the field in which you are deciding to go? Highlight that on your résumé. I have seen a few very innovative PowerPoint presentations that creatively chronicle the content on résumés as a second document to give an additional perspective to employers. A PowerPoint presentation is a great way to focus on the items of your business and brand about which you want a perspective client, sponsor, or company to know.

YouTube

YouTube is one of the most popular social media platforms

in the world, so it's a great place to build your brand and let your message be heard. Recording artists have launched successful careers on the back of their incredible YouTube fan base. Author and motivational speaker Eric Thomas, aka The Hip Hop Preacher, posts a video every Monday to empower his viewers to be their best. Thomas' desire to inspire others, coupled with his captivating weekly video messages, has helped him to amass a tremendous following, which led him to become a professional motivational speaker, an author, and the architect of an amazing legacy-building career.

Blog

We talked about how social media is a great means of engaging people and getting them to talk about your brand. But blogs, articles, and whitepapers are additional ways to demonstrate your knowledge in an industry or a specific topic. If you create a blog to help your brand, make sure that the content is in-line with your mission statement. Many college students have difficulty finding employment after graduation, which is why it's so important to begin building your brand before you start the job search or a new business.

When Lindsay Shoemaker was a college senior at Georgia College & State University in Milledgeville, GA, she decided to create her personal brand, after taking a class on branding. As a mass communications major, she enjoyed writing and started a blog called *That Working Girl*, which was intended to help young women considering the media industries as a career option. Although the site was doing well, it really took off when she began promoting it on her social media sites. Shoemaker was interning at a PR firm, and her employer was blown away by her effort — before they hired her. Take the time to make your voice heard via a blog.

Networking

Events, seminars, Lunch & Learns, and conferences are not intended to see how many cards you can give out or how many people you can meet. Instead they are about connecting with the right person with whom you can form a mutually beneficial relationship. If you are attending a conference you should research the people on the panels. Is there someone who could impact your career or take your business to another level? Conferences and networking events are fun and informative, but they should also be a place where you are connecting with people who will help expand your brand as well as expose it to people with whom you would not normally communicate. If someone is on a panel and you were not able to connect with them, Google them and see if they have a Twitter/Facebook account or website, and use one of those avenues to connect and possibly build a relationship with them.

Philanthropy

Personal branding is often seen as self-centered, but PCM helps you to realize philanthropy as a key component in fully developing yourself and how you impact others, and that means giving back to those who may not be able to help you. I was taught that when you feel down, you should help those who are having a harder time than you. It will change your perspective on your current situation. Giving back to your community is one way to show how important it is to you. If you are genuine about your efforts, those whom you serve will see your heart and, in return, will believe in you as well. By spending some time helping the people around you, you could be aiding the next CEO of a life-changing corporation. Do your part and you will help to change the world.

Earlier, I told you a story about my grandmother and how, I was amazed at all of the things she had done with her life. Mind you, she didn't receive tax deductions for her deeds and asked nothing in return for the lives she had impacted, but she did create a legacy. How can you create a legacy based on giving back to those in your community? I'm a firm believer that we should never leave a community the way we found it. We must do something to make it a better place.

Mentor

We each have a gift. Some of us are using our gifts in school and on the field, while others are displaying their gifts in the corporate arena or as an entrepreneur. Wherever, there's always someone whom you can encourage and mentor. Sometimes we take our gifts for granted, while others are in awe of what we can do with little effort. If you are able to impart knowledge to someone in need, imagine how you could change his or her life. Organizations, such as Year Up and National Peers Mentoring, are always looking for awesome mentors.

Create a nonprofit that serves a need in your community

We all have a talent that can be used to make a difference or a passion that drives us to help in a certain area. Why not use the assets we were either born with or acquired over time to create an organization that will positively impact lives? There are so many people in need of assistance and not enough organizations or resources to meet the need.

Serve on the board of directors of a nonprofit

Each of us has an expertise that is needed in some area or another. If you do not have the desire or drive to start a nonprofit, lend your skillset to an organization that is already in existence. There are several nonprofits looking for varied proficiencies and experience to help facilitate their mission. This will take minimal time, but could leave a major impact on the recipients.

Volunteer

One way to find out what a community needs is to volunteer. When you volunteer, you not only feel great for helping people, but you also gain a deeper understanding of how you can help the community-at-large. Your skillset or wisdom may be a key factor in changing or enhancing something within the community.

Changing one person's life by giving back could alter an entire community, or even the world. Consider the heroic, heartbreaking story of Malala Yousafzai, who stood up to the Taliban, risking her life as she advocated for the right of education for women. Even in the midst of an assassination attempt that led to her being hospitalized, it didn't stop her. Working even harder to share her story, Malala didn't shrink away in defeat or fear; her resilience ultimately took her to the U.N., where she called for worldwide access to education.

Brands that engage in giving back distinguish themselves from their competitors and see many benefits, including loyal customers and happier employees. This isn't just about enjoying personal success — it's about making your mark. It's about doing good for those around you. Once you have implemented your give-back plan, include it on your website so others can get involved as well.

BRANDERCISE

Finding your client/customer/team

Describe in detail your perfect client/customer or the industry/company within which you would like to work. If you want to be a physical trainer for a team, in what sport would you like to practice? Would it be for a professional sports team? What about the age group or the gender of the clients? How does this client or organization add value to your brand? Remember to be specific.

Chapter 14 : Manage Your Brand

"When you brand yourself properly, the competition becomes irrelevant."

— *Dan Schawbel*

Perception must equal reality. Your brand's core competencies should reflect exactly how your peers and people view you. You have spent so much time evaluating yourself and crafting a unique fingerprint that will help to catapult you to the next level, it would be a shame if you did not manage it. Personal brand management is an essential step in the branding and PCM process and is based on the decisions you make to strengthen your message, skills, and influence. In essence, it will determine the path your life takes and the type of legacy you leave.

In order to successfully manage your brand, you must continually answer the following questions: *What are people's perceptions of my brand? What must I keep doing in order to grow it? What should I start doing in order to enhance it? What are the things hurting my brand that I should stop immediately?* Although there are more detailed questions you can ask, these four will help you stay on track with who you are and where you are going as it pertains to your brand management. Additionally, you need to look at your mission statement and brand promise regularly to determine if you are still representing it.

What are people's perceptions of my brand?

A key component of brand management is being proactive and defining who you are and how you want to be known — rather than having others do it for you. Live your life making decisions that will positively impact your message. Oftentimes, in life and especially at work, we deal with many surprising and challenging issues that can sometimes throw us for a loop. If we don't handle them correctly and in a timely manner, we could destroy what we have worked so hard to develop. Stay the course of your brand and your beliefs.

I remember being a regional manager for a wireless company and having a vacant position that I was required to fill. I had the perfect person in mind, whom I had interviewed for a position just a few months prior. I was about to call and offer her the job, until I was told from within the company to consider another candidate. I agreed to interview this person, but I did not promise to hire her, unless she was the best candidate. My boss agreed. I had a face-to-face interview with her and two other candidates. Compared to the other two candidates, she was grossly unqualified.

I reported my findings to my boss and suggested not to hire her, because the other two candidates were more impressive and qualified. I was then informed that the person who wanted her to have the job decided to create another position, specifically to accommodate her. I stated my concern and was adamant about not hiring her, because the other candidates were a better fit. Ultimately, my boss strongly suggested I hire her due to internal pressure. In the end, I protected my reputation by standing my ground and refusing to bring on anyone who was not qualified. At the end of the day, she was not hired due to an HR issue.

Brand management is like a never-ending work-in-progress file and by staying on top of it, you will never fall behind. If you continuously work on your brand and remain true to yourself, you'll always be true to your brand and your perception will continue to reflect your reality. The best brand management people are those who keep the process simple. They know themselves and where they want to go, making it easy to share their vision with others. They spend time crafting specific messages that bring to light their mission statement. They have devoted brand ambassadors who understand their vision and are creative at devising messages, especially for their audience.

You know you are on the right track in developing your brand when you are attracting the right people and things in your life to help you advance it. Your pentagon will not only host all of the right people, but those who you attract will open doors you would have never even imagined. It's important you understand that when you stop managing your brand, your audience will find someone else who's doing something similar and follow them.

Personal brand management is being authentic to your followers and consistently promoting yourself and your destination — developing the plan to make your mission come true.

Here are 5 things to keep in mind when trying to successfully manage your brand:

1. Keep your brand unique: You discovered your one-of-a-kind qualities, traits, and skillsets when you were determining your purpose. Now it's time to put your ideas to the test. Promote your unique qualities in order to help you stand out among your competition.

2. Be answerable: It doesn't matter how many people you have working on your brand. It's yours, and you have the ultimate responsibility for its impact. That's why they call it *personal* branding. You should be in control of the overall message, whether it's disseminated via social media or personal interactions. Although you may have others overseeing it and suggesting directions, you must be committed to creating and managing it.

If there's an issue with your message, address it immediately.

3. Innovate yourself: How you are viewed (via how you have created and managed your personal brand), affect how you get jobs, sponsorships, or clients. What if, in the future, professional sports teams were to pick players with a strong personal brand as well as tremendous athletic ability? Take that one step further: What if the athlete who's better at the sport loses out because they have not spent time developing their brand? What your brand brings to the company, team, or school should be critical in helping the organization to grow. Clearly communicate and display all of your assets in order to be the one chosen for the role for which you are competing.

4. Be selective: If your message is crafted and managed correctly, people and companies will want to align themselves with you. But not everyone or everything is right for you. It's important to align yourself with people who are going to further enhance your message. Remember, correcting mistakes in brand management is harder than developing a brand in the first place, which is why athletes sometimes lose sponsorships when their status takes a dip due to legal troubles.

Don't neglect your ambassadors, associates, and others whom your brand is helping by partnering with people/ companies that don't align with your mission statement. When partnering think long-term; what might look good in the short-term may hinder you down the road. As you continue to grow, you need to seize opportunities that will help you meet your goals. Defining and clearly managing your brand are what allow you to navigate, course-correct, and seize the right opportunities.

5. Get Publicized: There is an old saying that all publicity is good publicity. That can be true only if it is managed correctly. Publicity, in general, positions you in front of potential customers, clients, or fans. However, if you happen to do something that hurts your brand and it is publicized, it will initially divert attention to your brand, but it is important that you work quickly to repair the damage. Make sure the increased number of people viewing your brand have an opportunity to see the authentic you.

Online management

Being proactive and keeping a watchful eye on your social media can be a full-time job. Luckily we have a few websites that can help with the process. Consider HootSuite, a social media dashboard that helps you to manage your posts and conversations (you're able to schedule posts for Twitter, Facebook, LinkedIn, Google+, Foursquare, MySpace, and Word Press). The ability to schedule posts will enable you to craft messages in advance that are in-line with your brand.

If you have been monitoring your Web presence and found erroneous tweets or embarrassing photos on social media sites, you'll need to begin the cleanup process right away. Go on each site and delete the messages. If someone else posted an objectionable message to your timeline, I would suggest emailing them and asking them to delete it. You can also ask search engines to remove the questionable posts.

Lastly, continue to monitor your Web presence by using tools such as Google Alerts and talkwalker.com. Both platforms generate notices based on search engine results, which are determined by criteria given by you, and deliver the results to your email or RSS feed.

BRANDERCISE

Brand monitoring

Go online and set up talkwalker.com alerts or Google Alerts, using your name. Both are free.

Chapter 15

Entrepreneur or Employee?

"Your time is limited, so don't waste it living someone else's life. Don't be trapped by dogma — which is living with the results of other people's thinking. Don't let the noise of others' opinions drown out your own inner voice. And most important, have the courage to follow your heart and intuition. They somehow already know what you truly want to become. Everything else is secondary."

— *Steve Jobs*

This is the point in Parallel Career Metamorphosis where people begin to waver in their decision to transition into their next life. Everything you have done up to this moment has been developing the best you possible. Now it is time to make the hard decision: Do I leave my comfortable, unsatisfying job to become an entrepreneur, start a new career, or move to another company? You can blame school, job, family, resources, finances, and the economy for only so long. Sooner or later, you have to realize that you and only you can create a new future for yourself. If you have a dream and you are not living it, or at least putting a plan in motion to follow your passion, then you are partly to blame.

Craig Valentine is currently a professional motivational speaker traveling around the world encouraging others to become speakers themselves. He has a phrase, "Do not let your good get in the way of your best," and he lives it out loud and proud. Craig was comfortable working at an Internet company, but his dream was to speak professionally around the world. He decided that he was going to take the plunge, so he met with his boss and told him that he would be leaving. His boss, in turn, told him he couldn't leave and that they were going to raise his salary. Craig replied that his decision was not a financial decision, but a dream decision. His boss then proceeded to raise his salary four more times; putting it well over six figures. Amazed at the offer, Craig told his boss that he had to think it over (i.e. he had to discuss it with his wife).

Upon hearing the story, his wife initially told him to take the money. But after thinking about it, she told Craig that his dream is not for sale. The next day, he went into the office and told his boss that he was leaving. His boss was disappointed, but Craig knew that he was doing the right thing, because that year he spoke professionally 160 times in four different countries. He was good at his job, but he is at his best when living his dream.

Change can be quite scary, especially for many people who attempt to start businesses after working long-term, full-time jobs. It's difficult to leave a great-paying position to transition to something that pays less but allows you to do what you love in an environment in which you can thrive. In this day and age, more people are being downsized or terminated due to the economy as well as innovation. Unfortunately, finding another job can be difficult due to a lack of transferrable skills or education. Creating a business of your own looks attractive when you can't find a job or are tired of working for someone else. It is important that you understand that starting a business is not for everyone.

For some students, choosing a major is hard enough; deciding if they're going to become entrepreneurs or follow in the footsteps of their parents and work at a corporation is terrifying. Choosing your career path is one of the most important decisions you will ever make. You want a career in which you not only thrive, but one that also allows you to wake up every morning with a smile on your face. If you make the right decision, it will positively impact all aspects of your life. Today, the average person will change career paths several times, and it's important to consider all of the factors that go into such a transition, including job security, financial stability, and the job market.

The great thing about making the entrepreneur/employee transition as a college student is that, in many cases, you have not incurred any debt, except in the event of student loans or credit cards. Whatever your choice, it might be a mistake or a blessing. Luckily, we can vet the decision and determine if your personality would be better suited for the lifestyle of an entrepreneur or employee. Here are a few things to consider:

Entrepreneurs are risk-takers. They opt for the road less traveled, while employees choose the newly paved highway. The bumpier road underscores entrepreneurs' determination, strength, and resilience to stay the course during times of uncertainty. Employees, on the other hand, are frequently afraid to fail, so they avoid entrepreneurs' risks.

In terms of completing the task at hand, entrepreneurs' and employees' execution varies drastically. Looking at the big picture, entrepreneurs create and determine a business' direction, profit, budgets, marketing, atmosphere, duties, and virtually everything else. However, employees have the leisure of allowing their employers to determine their income, schedule, workload, future, and benefits. One is active, the other passive.

As an employee, you receive directions regarding how to do your job, either directly or indirectly. You become accustomed to having your day-to-day actions administered by others. As an entrepreneur you determine your own actions, because doing so is the only way you'll get paid. If you don't market your business you won't get clients to buy your product or service. If you don't watch and understand your cash flow, then you may end up broke and looking for the next business opportunity or, quite possibly, a job.

When I worked as an account-marketing representative for a music distribution company, I had to visit independent retail locations each day to merchandise, as well as educate and train the owners. This sounds like a great opportunity, because I owned my own territory. I made my own hours and created my own schedule, plus I received free music and concert tickets to the best shows. It was a great job. However, one of my counterparts lasted only a week on the job, because he was not self-motivated and found it difficult to get up every morning, visit stores, and do what he was being paid to do. He needed someone over him and ended up quitting in order to find a 9-to-5 job.

As an employee you have clearly defined duties that you perform between 9 and 5. As an entrepreneur you have multiple jobs that have to be accomplished regardless of how long it takes. An entrepreneur's work schedule is nonstop. Yes, there are nights when they don't sleep. If something goes wrong, they have to handle it — unlike an employee, who has the option of blaming someone else or handing off the task if they don't feel like doing it themselves (depending on their job, of course). Unlike employees, entrepreneurs are typically the first to arrive at the office and the last to leave, particularly at startup. Additionally, entrepreneurs dislike weekends and holidays, but look forward to Mondays and other workdays, because they can do what they love to do — conduct business. Employees, on the other hand, live for the weekends, holidays, and anytime they can get off work.

As an employee you are usually assured of a paycheck on a consistent basis, whether it be monthly, bi-monthly, or weekly. An entrepreneur may have sporadic payments at the outset of their venture or if the business takes a turn for the worse. Growing and sustaining a business is all part of a juggling act that an entrepreneur must master in order to make their businesses successful. But when it does succeed it's one of the best feelings ever, because it's their venture — not someone else's.

Employees and entrepreneurs view vacations quite differently. Most employees can go on vacation with little to no thought of their job. But an entrepreneur is always thinking about their business, whether they are gone for a long weekend or an extended holiday. It's difficult to shut down, because they're always considering ways to grow and things that can go wrong. Entrepreneurs have more freedom to come and go as they please, because they make their own schedule, but their drive to be successful keeps them tied to the company and they rarely take breaks unless explicitly told to do so by their significant other.

Employees expect to have health insurance, a 401K, and other benefits in exchange for helping someone grow their company. Entrepreneurs, in contrast, supply those benefits to those whom they employ, which can be quite expensive. In the beginning, many entrepreneurs forgo benefits for themselves and contract work, so they're not obligated to pay for employee benefits. In essence an entrepreneur desires freedom, while an employee desires security.

Employees have very limited risk, because they are paid to do a service and as long as that service is completed per their job description they will be compensated. However, entrepreneurs are complete risk-takers, from creating to financing a business to working without knowing how consistently they will be paid. The unknowns of starting a business keep employees at their jobs, but the excitement of overcoming the unknowns, mastering the variables, and succeeding at being their own boss are the very makings of entrepreneurs.

Starting a business is a tremendous risk, because there's no assurance that your products or services will sell, or that your customers will pay their bills on time (if they pay them at all), or that your biggest client won't leave for a competitor. But there's simply nothing like success — it's a feeling you want to repeat with other ventures. Consider Oprah Winfrey: Although she had a successful TV show, she felt it was time to create something of her own (no pun intended), so she developed OWN, a network that allows her to craft a unique slate of programming. It seems that almost everything Oprah's been involved with turns to gold, but this is the case only because she works so very hard and is willing to take risks to make it happen.

An entrepreneur must have focus that will keep them on course no matter the obstacle. Jay-Z is a perfect example because of his broad, unprecedented success as a rapper and businessman. He has platinum albums, sold-out concerts, a clothing line in top stores, a well-known restaurant, a sports agency, and much more. He made the decision to not waste his time on anything that would not expand his legacy. For instance, when *Forbes* staff writer Zack O'Malley Greenburg requested that Jay-Z be a part of the book that he was writing about him, he declined, because he was busy pursuing other ventures. He later published his own book, garnering all of the profits.

Understanding the difference of being an entrepreneur versus an employee enables a person to determine which path is better suited to them. Making such a decision puts you at a crossroads in your life; you must decide if you are going to go to the left or the right. There's no correct or incorrect answer, because both roads will get you to your desired destination. You just have to figure out how you are going to get there by realizing what will make you happier and more fulfilled.

The big question: Should you become an entrepreneur or an employee?

Chapter 16

Becoming an Entrepreneur

"What do you need to start a business? Three simple things: Know your product better than anyone. Know your customer, and have a burning desire to succeed."

— *Dave Thomas*

Becoming a successful entrepreneur is a marathon, although not a typical marathon composed of 26 miles of predictable terrain. No, an entrepreneurial marathon is littered with unknown obstacles that stand between you and achieving your goals. Such a marathon can be a frightening yet exhilarating experience. Imagine leaving the security of a job to start your own business, with all of its pitfalls and uncertainties. If the business fails, you could experience financial and psychological setbacks. If the business succeeds, you'll have the joy of experiencing your dream come true, the freedom of running it the way you see fit, and numerous financial rewards.

Entrepreneurs start with a dream — to create a business that will positively impact the community. Success demands that you have unyielding drive regardless of circumstance, patience when things are not going as expected, and a deeply held belief in what you are creating. A new business requires discipline, because other visionaries have followed their dreams and developed a similar entity that failed, but you have to find the missing ingredient that will set your business apart so that it stands the test of time.

Researching, planning, and unwavering determination to succeed got you into your dream university, or drafted by the professional sports team, or the job that was supposed to go to someone else. It's your clear vision that helps you to make crucial decisions that keep your doors open when others are closing. As an entrepreneur, your marathon is most difficult, because everything that needs to be done is up to you. The upside is that when your business succeeds, you'll be a stronger person, financially, mentally, and physically.

A true entrepreneur will never be happy working a job. Why? Because they would seldom enjoy as much freedom, income, or personal gratification as by making their dream a reality. In order to do this, you must be self-motivated. There are so many people who say they want to be entrepreneurs, but they do nothing about it. Some of your friends have great ideas . . . absolutely amazing ideas . . . so much so, you find yourself thinking, *Dang, I wish I thought of that*. The problem is that they do nothing with the idea. Then, a few months or years later, they see someone else making their idea a reality.

An entrepreneur has to wake up every morning and make things happen. I'm sure you have friends who are forever creating a plan, but it never seems to come to fruition. As an entrepreneur you have to come up with the idea, create a plan, and then put the plan into action. If you are not going to act on the idea, please go and fill out an application for a job, because you need someone to tell you what to do, when to do it, and how to do it. An entrepreneur has to act smartly and swiftly. Failure to do so may result in losing an opportunity to start a business or to take a business to the next level.

Becoming a student entrepreneur

We spend a lot of time focusing on entrepreneurs who are transitioning from 9-to-5 employees to self-employed business owners. But what about the non-traditional jobs, where people are still considered employees but they don't fall under the 9-to-5 description, such as a professional athlete, a pilot, or a student (my mom always told me that school was my job)?

Whether you are starting a business while you are still in school, playing a professional sport, or working a traditional 9-to-5, the thought of actually doing it can be scary and the process daunting. People frequently start a business by taking on a few projects, if they have a skill or expertise for which someone will pay. If you do start your business this way, it will take you longer to get going because you still have to make sure that you are doing your best at your 9-to-5. However, it will give you the financial security that you (and, quite likely, your family) need in order to make that transition.

As we discussed earlier, there's very little loyalty left in corporate America. As you are building your business your boss could be planning his/her own exit to another company. While I was working for the wireless company, I was transparent about my own business. I told my supervisors exactly what I was doing and that it didn't conflict with their company's business, so I was allowed to continue. They also knew that the pay I was receiving was inadequate to cover my expenses and that I might require additional income to sustain my lifestyle — in other words, it was a win-win.

We find all kinds of reasons to stop us from doing what we're supposed to be doing, and transitioning from employee to entrepreneur is no exception.

- ☞ **A stable job market:** The economy will always be unpredictable, even in a good market, and if you build and maintain your personal brand you should be able to beat out your competitors for a job if you choose to be an employee again.

- ☞ **Irreplaceable:** We feel like we're irreplaceable, but if you leave your job today, know that within two weeks they'll have someone else in your place. In most jobs, you are replaceable in less time than you think.

- ☞ **Finances:** We never have enough savings to leave our jobs. If you believe in your dream and you are a true entrepreneur, you will do everything in your power to make your business work. See to it that you have six months to a year's worth of savings before you leave the job. You will always have bills and unexpected expenses to take care of, but if you plan and budget correctly, you'll hopefully be able to take care of them. This is not the money you are using to start the business, but rather the money you'll live on.

☞ **Bad timing:** There's never a great time to leave your job, because there's always another bonus, pay increase, or fire drill that needs your attention. But you'll give yourself all of these rewards and more, so stop awaiting their rewards/perks and develop your own within your company.

☞ **Friends:** You should go into any business believing that you are going to succeed, but you must also realize that 50% of businesses fail within the first year and 95% within the first five years, so be emotionally and financially prepared for that possibility. You may not get the support you expect from friends and family, because they do not understand your vision. *You must believe in yourself, because there will be times when no one else will, and when things are not looking good you have to believe that they will work out.*

You have made the decision to become an entrepreneur. Now you must formulate your exit strategy using these 8 guidelines:

1. Business plan: From the point of business-concept inception to leaving your current job, you must have a plan. A business plan contains all of the details, from location (if you are going to have one), to marketing your product or service, to the finances you'll need to make it all happen. After you have written a business plan, formulate an exit strategy that includes a timeline specifying how you'll bring this business to life. While planning will not prevent unforeseen circumstances, it will help you recover faster and easier because you are prepared.

2. Mentor/advisor: Enlist the help of your mentor/ advisor to guide you through the process, support you when the process feels overwhelming, and be a sounding board for ideas and other things that will arise. A mentor and/or advisor will be invaluable in helping you make a smooth transition from *employee* to *entrepreneur*.

3. Transition education: Do you know your company's policy about working additional jobs? If you are in a non-traditional 9-to-5 or are a student, you probably don't have to worry about such a policy. However, if you are in a traditional 9-to-5 you should be aware that working on other businesses is usually against company policy, and you could be written up or even lose your job as a result. Be aware, and be ready for the consequences if there are any. *Investigate your company's rules and regulations regarding working another job or having your own company.*

4. Time management: Maximize your time as an employee by completing projects early but to the best of your ability. This might allow you time to work on your own business while on company time and still meet your deadlines. As an entrepreneur you may be contracted to do a job. Note: Be careful that you are not caught using company resources to do it. As a student or non-traditional employee you want to utilize the time not spent studying or working to complete tasks for your new business. It's just as important to make sure that the contracted work is your best and that it's finished way ahead of deadline, so your clients are impressed and would possibly extend your contract or refer you to other potential clients. *Develop a timeline that highlights all of the tasks that you need to complete and then devise a schedule to accomplish them.*

5. Do not tell: It would be bad practice to solicit coworkers to sell your product or service, especially if you are not certain of your company's second-job policies. As a student or non-traditional employee, you are free to utilize the people around you, but I would encourage you to first develop clients outside of your circle. Unfortunately, not everyone within your circle will be happy about your new venture; they may try to discourage you, tell management (which could lead to your dismissal), or talk negatively about you to others, discouraging them from being clients. *The less you tell coworkers about your new venture the better. Find clients/ customers outside of your work environment.*

6. Financially fit: If your business is a success, the first thing you'll want to do is quit your job/school in order to work on it full-time. Make sure you have a least six to 12 months of personal savings set aside before you leave your steady source of income. If you are a student, get your degree. There are tons of examples of successful people (Zuckerberg, Jobs, Gates) who have left school and succeeded in business. But if you are close to finishing, why not add a degree to your list of accomplishments? *Using your current salary, devise a budget by which you're putting money away for your personal savings as well as your prospective business (you'll be your first investor). Live below your means and pay off any outstanding debt.*

7. Employee 20%/Entrepreneur 80%: You know it's time to leave when you feel that the job is hindering you from doing what needs to be done for your business. If you used to say "yes" to additional work, but now you're declining, or if you're arriving at 10:00 am instead of 9:00

am while leaving at 4:30 pm instead of 6:30 pm, then the writing is on the wall. On Mondays you were frequently seen at the water cooler, discussing the past weekend's highlights. Now you rarely leave your desk. As a matter of fact, you're checking your employee email and voicemail less frequently, because you are busy working on your new business. *It's definitely time for you to leave because you don't want your job to suffer. You have a stellar brand at the company and you want to leave with it very much intact.*

8. A professional goodbye: When you decide to leave your job, make sure to do so in a manner in which you can return if you so choose, or do it so that if there's a way to generate business from them, you'll be their first choice. Burning bridges doesn't help anyone. Before you leave make sure that your boss, coworkers, and possible clients know where to find you and what you'll be doing. *Leave the door open if you want to go back or if you need help. But in your mind, close the door for good, so when times get hard you don't consider throwing in the towel and going back to the 9-to-5.*

Being an entrepreneur is not for everyone, because corporations incentivize employees who are intrapreneurs (i.e. an employee who's given autonomy to develop new business or services within the context of the company). For those of you who want to remain in your corporate roles and only want to add to your skillset, remember that most companies reward intrapreneurs who help them grow a brand by devising or launching improvements. If you have the entrepreneurial spirit and decide you want to stay at your company and build a new brand or service, know that you could be rewarded but that your contributions will never leave with you should you choose to go elsewhere. Your innovations and improvements belong to the company for which they were created.

Chapter 17

The Company Mindset

"First, you have to be passionate about your business, because having your own business is not a job — it is a way of life. Second, create (and articulate) your vision for the business, and then be relentless in executing your go-to-market strategies and tactics. A solid plan is important; hard work and execution are critical."

— *Tom Nieman*

Your personal brand is the catalyst that guided you through the PCM process. It's time to utilize your brand to complete the transition and build your company. It will help you to mold your new work environment, aid in securing your first client/customer, and assist in the marketing of your company. Creating your new entity begins with a business plan to give you clarity, direction, and financing (if necessary). Below you'll find an outline of a typical business plan; you can go online to SBA.gov or other sites to glean more details. Although the entire plan is critical, I have highlighted certain portions to which you should pay particular attention.

When you start your business, as an entrepreneur you will wear all of the hats. But as it grows, you will want to populate it with leaders who are building their own brands. People who care about building their brand care about building the company for which they are working, so that everyone involved succeeds. Make sure your team is collaborative, so that you are getting the best out of them. The more you trust them to do what you hired them to do, the more you'll be able to see the big picture and quickly recognize/adapt to necessary changes. It will also help you to provide better products or services, which, in turn, will build a stronger organization. If you assist your team in being the best they can be, you will get the best out of your employees. And if they leave your organization, your brand will actually become stronger because you would have helped nurture them to go out on their own and succeed. By living your brand and enabling others to live theirs, you are impacting their lives; they, in turn, will impact others' lives, perpetuating the cycle and changing a community.

Setting the tone of your work environment and choosing the right employees are important steps in creating a successful business. It goes without saying that you must have a needed product or service, and location is key, but if you don't have winning employees you will have an uphill battle. As you build your business you will be developing a goal-oriented, like-minded, supportive team that must believe in you and your dream. If they do, they will work hard, much like your ambassadors.

As with picking your pentagon, when selecting your employees you will initially want to utilize your friends and family. We love and value the people in our lives. Some of them have been with us since the beginning. Still, this does not mean that they are the right fit for the next stage in your business life. Ideally all of your employees should be leaders, building their own brands. If they do not have a personal-brand mindset (being excellent at whatever they do and creating excellence wherever they are), they may be the right fit even though they might not want to start their own business. Rather, it means that they know themselves, where they are going, and how they can help you utilize their assets for your success.

Years ago, I initiated a business with a couple of friends. We had a great dynamic, each of us bringing different skills to the table. However, one of us did not understand the initial budgets of a start-up. She thought each of us would take home upwards of $100,000 by the end of the year. We had to explain to her that we were probably not going to bring in $100,000 total during the first year. She then requested to be paid first, as she had to deal with some overdue bills. The rest of the group, who understood the life and obligations of entrepreneurship, was quite taken aback. We all had bills and knew that we would have to budget for the first year in order to make the business succeed. We realized that the arrangement was not going to work out, because not all of us had the entrepreneurial mindset. In the end, we did not move forward with the business, but we became great friends. This person's personal brand is incredible and, in other circumstances, she excels.

Marketing

Having a great business product or service, and not telling anyone about it, is a waste of time and money. Let the world know who you are and what you have to help them. In marketing your company you will also be marketing your brand. Depending upon your product or service, you will most likely be the face of the company — the person whom prospective clients/customers meet when they walk in your door. You have spent so much time telling the world the ways in which you are an expert in your field; if your new business is within the same industry, use it to garner the attention of potential clients/customers. However, there may come a time when you'll have to choose between building your brand and your company's brand. If this is one of many businesses you'll be building, continue to expand your brand. However, if this company is turning into the next Apple or Nike, you may want to build the company's brand, maintaining your brand only to help the company grow.

Initially, you will want to research your target market in order to connect with the correct customer/client. If you put them first, they will always give you the necessary information to grow your business. You can survey your current customers/clients to get vital feedback regarding the pros and cons of your product/service. If they see that you value their feedback, they will perceive their own value and become a brand ambassador for both you and your product/service. As we discussed earlier, word-of-mouth is the very best marketing.

Continue to broadcast to the world that *you* have a new business and give them updates: sales, product launches, education, accomplishments, and awards. Do this via the company's website or newsletters, as well as your own personal social media sites. In the beginning, your credentials will bring you customers/clients, but as your business grows you must determine if your brand needs to move behind the scenes or stand out front to drive sales.

When marketing your company, start with the typical collateral (business cards, postcards/flyers, website, letterhead, envelopes). But you should also engage in traditional advertising (billboards, magazines, radio, TV) and utilizing online tools (Twitter, Facebook, YouTube, blogs). No matter the vehicle, communicate with your customers, because they're the only way you'll stay in business. Many people think, *If I have a great product or service, my customers/clients will come.* But that's not entirely true. It also takes a great marketing strategy to attract them. However, customer service combined with a terrific product will keep them *coming back.*

Community Engagement

Make an impact within your community and you will win over customers. Throughout the PCM process you have heard how important it is to give back. Well, in developing a sound business, it is equally important to change your community for the better. Utilizing existing events to demonstrate how your entity will help the community is not only a great way to brand, but also a terrific means of showing that you care and that you are an integral part of the community as well. Another purpose for events is to have attendees learn something about your business and for you to learn something about your potential clients/customers. Do not forget to follow-up with those who attended your event to see how you can be of service to them.

1. Business Description
   a. Business Type
   b. Products/Services
   c. Online/Brick-and-Mortar
      i. Location
   d. Business Overview
      i. Why this business
      ii. Why it will be successful

2. Personnel, Management, and Operations
   a. Owners and Their Bios
   b. Organization Chart
   c. Licenses, Permits
   d. Product Development
   e. Start-Up Plan

3. Sales and Marketing
   a. Business Specialty
   b. Market Size and Growth Trends
   c. Competition Analysis
   d. Marketing
   e. Sales Development Activity

4. Finances
   a. Staring Expenses
   b. Income Statement
   c. Cash Flow Projections
   d. Balance Sheet
   e. Application for Funding
      i. Income Statement Projections
      ii. Start-Up Balance Sheet

Chapter

18 : A Branded Career

> "Unless you have absolute clarity of what your
> brand stands for, everything else is irrelevant."
> — *Mark Baynes*

A **well-crafted personal brand creates opportuni-**
ties in any job market. It opens doors that may have
been closed. It gets you in front of decision-makers.
If Howard Schultz were looking for a job, he would have more
people calling him than he could possibly entertain. Who's
Howard Schultz? He's the founder of Starbucks. The journey
to his present position was not an easy one. Schultz was raised
in a Brooklyn housing project, but he excelled in football and
received an athletic scholarship to Northern Michigan University. A few years after graduating, he landed a marketing job
at a local coffee bean store called Starbucks. While there, he
traveled to Italy and was inspired to open a coffee café in the
U.S. Upon his return, he suggested the idea to his bosses, but
they declined. A determined Schultz opened a rival shop also
called Starbucks that made coffee with the Starbucks beans. His
company was so successful that he bought Starbucks from his
old supervisors a couple of years later for $3.8 million. In 1992

Starbucks went public, and it's been growing remarkably ever since. Schultz is a prime example of building and living your brand through excellence and innovation. Today, he continues to define his brand and inspire others by investing in business ventures.

When looking for work or seeking a new opportunity, the first thing most people do is create a résumé, and there's nothing wrong with that. But it's just as important to make sure that your personal brand is telling your story. A résumé is great for networking or applying for jobs, but you can also utilize LinkedIn or your own personal website to tell the world who you are and what you are doing to make your mark. To conduct an efficient job search you must know yourself, what you want, and understand how to best position yourself in front of decision-makers. The days of walking your résumé into a corporate office and possibly speaking to a decision-maker or HR person are long gone; a company's first impression of you is your résumé or social media profile. In today's job market it comes down to knowing and communicating your brand, so that you can land the position you want.

If you have gone through the job-seeking process, you know what you have to do: Create a résumé, begin networking, submit your résumé to job sites and companies; then execute more networking and, lastly, interview. Hopefully there will be only one interview, but oftentimes several interviews are required to land your desired position. The aforementioned process has become more streamlined due to technology.

Developing and managing your brand will help you to take some of the stress out of the job-search process, because you will have been delivering a consistent message that can be followed. Your ambassadors will help to get the word out about you and may even connect you with your next employer. Your brand will help you to stand out among your competition. However, as more and more people develop a brand strategy you'll have to work harder to make sure you are the best at what you do.

We no longer rely on just résumés. Our résumé opens the door, but our brand sells us by delivering a clear message containing our unique value proposition. A résumé cannot simply be a piece of paper listing your education, employment history, and capabilities. It must make clear who you are, as well as mention your skills/strengths and how they're relevant to the job. If you have done your research, you have incorporated key words from the job description, so that Web crawlers can pick your résumé out of hundreds.

Another key to developing a winning résumé is to make sure that it accurately reflects the brand you portray in person and on social media. Your brand must be consistent across all platforms. If you take a look at several résumés and compare them to their authors' respective social media profiles, you may see conflicting educational backgrounds, employment histories, and capabilities. Although it would be ideal if they were identical, it's OK if they're not, as long as they're accompanied by a strong brand message and a story that weaves all of those conflicts together. As we discussed earlier, a brand is a story. If you can describe your experiences in a way that creates a seamless narrative and then explain how your history will help the company, you'll win. Know your brand and your story. For example, Howard Schultz has a clear, concrete story of his humble beginnings and early innovations that changed the way we all think about coffee.

Social media is a necessary tool in the job-search process, because your prospective employer will research those outlets to see if your brand is consistent with your résumé. Social media should draw an even more detailed picture of your brand, because it allows you to express yourself in ways that a résumé doesn't. Make sure that the messaging (verbiage, photos, and overall content) is consistent.

When you are looking for a job, you must network with people in your industry. Your résumé and social media will help you to land an interview or even the job itself, but there's nothing better than meeting someone and giving them a firsthand look and feel of your brand. If it's authentic, the person you meet will walk away with a great impression, and your résumé/social media profiles will reinforce their experience.

Additionally, your introductions will be seamless, because the people who know your brand also know what you want to do and are qualified to do moving you one step closer to that interview. As we all know, an interview is a moment when you put your best foot forward so that a prospective employer can see how you communicate your brand. It's where it all comes together, giving you an opportunity to showcase your message visually and verbally. You need to dress the part. Your look needs to be consistent with your brand, but it must also adhere to typical interview rules of appearance. Verbally you should restate what's on your résumé and social media profiles, so that your brand is consistent. If you rely on a list of qualifications alone, nothing will stand out. But if you tell a compelling story that creates an emotional attachment, you will be setting yourself apart.

If Howard Schultz were being interviewed for a job, and he told his recruiter about the time he went to his supervisors with a great idea but they declined, imagine what the recruiter would think: *Here's a guy who comes up with great ideas and is not scared to bring them to management.* They would also like the fact that he believed in his idea so much that he made it happen. There's always some nugget in a résumé that you can expound upon with a compelling story. When I worked as a regional manager, I was interviewing a candidate who highlighted in her résumé the fact that she spoke Spanish and planned events. However, during her interview she downplayed those skills and I hired another candidate. I later discovered that she was behind some very big events in the market and spoke Spanish fluently. Had she told me a captivating story about her history, I probably would've given her the job. She didn't know her brand or brand story well enough to sell herself. Throughout the interview, you must be confident and never exaggerate (lie), because in doing so you will be untrue to your brand. You do not need to be anything other than who you are, because you are just living your brand.

Identifying and managing your brand before you begin a job search can make the process easier, because you will have a more cohesive approach. But in no way does it guarantee you the job. It should, however, enable you to communicate your brand in a manner that helps you stand out among other qualified candidates. After you receive the job of your dreams you *must* show your excellence. You worked hard to build your brand, to get the coveted job — now it's time to show them what you can do. Let your actions support the words on your résumé. Rise through the ranks of your company and/or your industry based upon your brand distinction. What you do with your career will be the legacy you leave behind.

Chapter 19

Legacy Building

> "Own your legacy each day.
> Each second. Each minute. Each hour.
> They never come back. Tomorrow is not an
> action, it's an excuse.
> Today, indeed this moment, is when you need
> to build your legacy.
> Today, indeed this moment, is when you
> become the person you want to be.
> Today, the day is short don't waste a moment."
> — *Anna Farmery*

You have crafted your ideal authentic brand and are working hard to maintain it, because it will be the cornerstone of your legacy. The world will remember your brand and everything you associate it with. Michael Jackson worked his entire life to carve out an unforgettable brand of excellence, through both timeless music and stunning performances. We may not have the same talents as Michael, but we're each gifted in our own way. So it's important that we make a mark that will last long after we have left this earth.

Unfortunately, far too many people consider the details of

their legacy only when they're dying. We should all be thinking about the type of legacy we'll leave while we're busy living. What exactly is a legacy? A legacy is defined as anything handed down from the past, as from an ancestor or predecessor. "Anything" could be a reputation (personal brand), a business, or personal assets. As it pertains to your legacy, what do you do in every stage of your life? What's your contribution to society on a personal level? What's your mark, in terms growth and innovation within the business world? Your legacy flourishes as you live your brand to the fullest. Find a solution to a problem, disrupt the status quo, or inspire others to see something through to fruition. A legacy is a vision and strategy that creates a *lasting future*, turning *inspiring vision* into an *actionable marketing strategy*.

When we discuss legacies, we're talking about two separate things: your reputation (beliefs, work ethic, and community involvement) and your property (personal/financial assets that you'll leave to family, friends, and the world).

If, after you have developed your personal brand and have decided to become an entrepreneur, you will hopefully have a business legacy to leave future generations. (If you work as an employee you will also leave a legacy.) It's important that you consider this legacy — which does not mean that you do things based upon the legacy, but that you have developed an authentic brand with which all of your decisions and actions fall in-line. As we discussed earlier, Michael Jackson was the epitome of a personal brand while he was alive and after he

Angela Mayartis Johnson is a dynamic motivational speaker, author and entrepreneur who successfully redefined her brand from Music Marketing Executive to Personal Brand Development Specialist and coach. Through her marketing company, Twenty6markting and Management, she focuses on helping individuals discover their passion, brand their niche and build their legacy. She founded Mayartis Brand Academy, as a speaking/training forum, where she uses clearly defined and applicable techniques to passionately empower attendees to overcome fears, realize their dreams and make their distinctive mark on the world.